You can do it!

Make Money
With Horses

Other books by Don Blazer

The Match
Walter Spills The Oats
Natural Western Riding
Training Performance Horses
Healthy Horses Seldom Burp!
Training the Western Show Horse
Nine Secrets of Perfect Horsemanship
Horses Don't Care About Women's Lib

The know and Go Series of E-Booklets:
Bits, Simple, Yet Effective
Nutrition: Science and Observation
Horse Training Is Horse Talking
Conformation: Form and Function
Is He Shod Right?

www.donblazer.com

You Can Do It!

Make Money With Horses

Don Blazer

Revised Edition
Editor: Meribah Small

Success Is Easy, Scottsdale, Arizona
www.donblazer.com

Published by: **Success Is Easy**
7119 East Shea Blvd.
Suite 109-271
Scottsdale, AZ 85254
www.donblazer.com

First published as a **Success Is Easy** paperback 1998
Revised in 2000
Second Printing 2000
Third Printing 2001
Revised in 2002
Fourth Printing 2003

Library of Congress Catalog Card Number 97-92440

ISBN 0-9660127-0-4

Printed in the United States of America

Table of Contents

Warning--Disclaimer

Introduction
It's business. It's you.

Horses can make you a lot of money.

You can realize a good living with horses, raise a family, and send the kids to college. Horses can even provide a very nice nest egg for retirement.

That isn't wishful thinking, or a crazy claim made just to get your attention. It is fact.

This book doesn't make wild claims or unattainable promises. This book presents facts and directions. Every horse sale example in this book is verifiable; it's all on record.

If you like horses, and want them to make money for you, then this book is for you. If you like horses, but aren't interested in making money with them, buy one of my other books. My other books are all about the thrills and excitement of riding, training and caring for horses.

This book only explains how horses can make money, profits, income. This isn't a long book, nor a complicated one. The matter of making money isn't complicated, nor does it need a lengthy explanation.

And you don't have to get lucky to make money. Making money with horses simply requires that you understand where the opportunities for profits lie, that you can make unemotional business decisions, and that you are willing to dedicate yourself to reaching your goals. These are the same factors required to make money in any business.

There are a lot of statistics in this book. While the statistics are facts, they do get outdated. So, don't view the statistics as absolutes. View them as guides--your guides to profit opportunities. Use the guide which applies and make some logical business decisions. Realize statistics change daily, and that if you do some updating now and then, you'll see new and better opportunities for making money with horses. Envision where your business will be in 10 years, and try to make that vision a reality today.

Choose the breed you like best, because it doesn't really matter what breed of horse you fancy. You can make money with any breed. (Now, I will admit and you will have to accept the fact that some breeds are more popular than others, so each breed presents opportunities for profit in different ways.)

It doesn't matter the age or sex of the horses. There is a way to make money with stallions, mares, weanlings, yearlings and older horses.

And it doesn't matter which area of the horse business you choose. You can make money as an owner, breeder, broker, syndicator or a trainer.

Are there risks?

Of course. There are risks to everything. The only certainty is uncertainty. But the risks become inconsequential when you make the choice to accept the uncertainties of life and give up any desire for the impossible notion of security.

As with every other investment venture, making money with horses takes some work, knowledge, skill, self-control and thought. Along the way there will be some heartaches and some disappointments, but there will be just as many joys and big profits--30, 40, 50 or 100 per cent return on investment in weeks, months, or less than a year. That's common. A 300, 400 or 500 percent return is not uncommon!

It is simple. Horses can make you money this year, and even more next year, because horses are an exciting, fast-moving, personal involvement, open-to-anyone business.

But there are rules which must be followed. Some are hard; some are not so hard.

If you allow your emotions to influence your decisions, or you think you can ignore or violate any of the rules, forget making money.

The first absolute rule is: CHOOSE WHAT YOU LIKE DOING BEST, BECOME EXPERT AT IT, AND DON'T LEAVE YOUR AREA OF EXPERTISE.

Sounds easy, but it's hard.

You'll know when you strayed from your area of expertise. A little loss will show up on your next profit/loss statement.

If you love horses and make them your life's work, that is a richness of its own.

If you love horses and want to make them your business, and you follow the rules of this workbook, horses can make you a lot of money.

So let's get started.

**Everyone has a unique talent.
Discover your talent, use it, and all
you do will be both easy and successful.**

Chapter one
Do what you love to do!

If horses aren't making you a lot of money right now, but you want them to make money, then you'll have to change your ways.

It may be difficult, but it is essential you accept the fact that making money with horses is a business. You must understand that a business is an occupation, a profession, a trade. A business is that with which one is principally and very seriously concerned. A business is a planned activity. It is not a few hours of furious work when the mood strikes you--that is a foolish waste of energy.

A business is the purchase or production of goods, followed by the sale of the merchandise in an attempt to make a profit. A business is providing a service for a fee.

A horse business is not buying any old horse just because you've always wanted one. It is not keeping a horse in your backyard, feeding it carrots and riding it down the trail with friends.

A business is not loving a horse--although the love of horses will make your business much more successful.

A horse business is the breeding of horses, the racing of horses, the training of horses and the sale of horses with the intention of making a profit. Making money with horses is doing one of those things (choose the one you like doing best), and doing it better than most other people.

You can do it! And you can make money doing it!

Choose any facet of the horse business. There are lots of different things you can do with horses. Simply choose to do it with the commitment of making a profit, and if you follow the rules outlined in this book, you will make a profit.

Ownership of horses with any motive in mind other than the making of a profit will be stamped "hobby" by the Internal Revenue Service. "Hobby" horses won't make you money. Hobbies cost you money.

What kind of horses will make money?

All kinds and every kind.

Why? Because more and more people want to own horses. The market is constantly growing, and it is constantly expanding in new directions. It has been calculated that nearly 80 per cent of the people involved with horses are new to the horse industry every four years. That's a lot of new people who need everything from a new horse to a new trainer.

Back in the 1920s, the horse was a work animal. He was at his peak of usefulness and he was at his peak of population in the United States, or so it was thought. However, as the need for work horses began to decline, so did the number of horses. A farmer didn't want a horse if the horse didn't work. Horses simply weren't of any value if they couldn't produce an income or **satisfy a need**. (Always keep the **"satisfy a need"** idea in mind--it is what propels your business.)

By the 1950s, the horse was out of a job, and therefore the United States government decided he was no longer of any interest. The government stopped counting horses on a regular basis, and it stopped including the horse in research programs which received federal funds. As usual, government was reacting to a situation which had already passed and would never be seen again. As usual, while government was working at being ineffective and unable to see the future, the horse was beginning to gallop in all kinds of new directions.

The bureaucrats did not understand that the horse and mankind have had a love affair since their initial meeting, and that mankind will never abandon the horse.

Like a Phoenix rising from the ashes of the work horse, a new type of horse and owner emerged on the scene-- the pleasure-horse and his owner.

The pleasure-horse owner saw way beyond the useful work animal. The pleasure-horse owner saw then, and sees now, beauty and grace, a faithful friend, a return to the romance of days long gone, a challenge to the future. He has a great pride in his horse for any number of reasons, and that pride has expanded into other new worlds--recreation and competition.

So while the number of horses was actually declining, the demand for a new kind of horse was rapidly increasing. And you know how much business loves "an ever increasing demand."

Everything was booming in the United States in the 1960s and 70s, and so were all phases of the horse industry. As people had more expendable income, they spent more on their horses. Competition became increasingly keen in all aspects of horse sport. Trail and recreational riding were growing at twice the rate of competition riding.

With growing national affluence, horse-owning Americans found themselves enjoying everyday activities which once had been only for the rich. Americans were showing at halter, playing polo, fox hunting, show jumping, and yes, engaging in the sport of kings--racing horses.

When the horse went from a work animal to a pleasure animal, the please and competition horse business exploded into a multi-billion dollar industry. And the value of horses skyrocketed with the moon shots.

But an idea which had been dead for nearly 25 years was still driving the price of horses. People still said a horse's value was tied to his potential to work or earn an income. Of course, the horse wasn't working and he had little chance--except for race horses--to produce cash flow. When the average horse buyer suddenly recognized reality, the bubble of high prices for horses burst, and the horse industry suffered a staggering decline in the 80s. The price of horse's dropped to zero, breeders when bust, and most trainers contemplated suicide or taking a "real" job in town.

But the downturn didn't last long as a new dose of reality put the price of horses on a new flight toward the stars.

There are two parts to the new reality. First, horses aren't cheap to raise or train; so if you want a well-bred horse well trained, you are going to have to pay. Second, when someone wants that horse they are willing to pay the price no matter how high. There is no longer a price ceiling on horses.

Today, there is absolutely no standard by which to measure the actual value of a horse.

A horse is worth what someone is willing to pay, not actually for the horse, but for the satisfaction of their desire as represented by that horse (potential). And believe me, people are willing to pay "whatever it takes."

There has never been a more exciting time in the horse industry, and there has never been a more opportune time to make money with horses.

The single idea that a person is willing pay whatever it takes to get the potential satisfaction represented by a horse virtually guarantees you can't do anything but make money with horses.

If you are determined to make money with horses, and you follow the rules in this book, you will be successful!

Just to get a glimpse of how big the business of horses is, and how much potential there is for horses to make you a lot of money, let's look at some statistics.

Back in the early 1950s, the U.S. horse population was estimated at approximately 3.5 million. In those days no one bothered to estimate the dollar impact of the horse industry. It was just too small.

Best estimates, according to the American Horse Council, Washington D. C., put the 2002 horse population at about 8 million. California listed at two plus million horses; Texas, over one million.

And the contribution of the United States horse industry to the Gross National Product is now estimated at well above $27 billion.

With 250 million persons in the country, the American Quarter Horse Association (AQHA) transferred nearly 250,000 horses in one year. That's one horse, or one transaction, for every 500 people in the United States. You are sharp in your mathematics if you immediately figured 250,000 transactions for 250 million people should be one transaction for every 1,000 people. But it takes two to tango and two to trade a horse; so there were two parties involved in each transaction, or sale--so let's make it one for every 500.

You can also argue, if that's what you want to do, that many, many horseowners have more than one horse. It's true, and a good point. It is also true the 250 million Americans living in this country are grouped into families of which there are mothers, fathers, and children of varying ages all the way down to infancy. This cuts the number of "active participants" drastically. If you just divided eight million horses into the total population, it would translate into one horse for every 32 persons. So, let's drop that point until a little later. We can nit-pick figures all day. The point is there are a lot more horses and a lot more people involved with horses than first meets the eye--that is NOW a fact.

Assume there are 10 breed associations with comparable registrations to the AQHA. Of course, we know the AQHA is the largest by far, but it is only one of no less than 142 active registries in the United States. So let's say all the others combined make 10 of equal size to the AQHA. If there were 10 times the number of annual transactions made by

AQHA, then one person in every 50 in the U.S. would be involved with horses in one way or another. These figures offer staggering possibilities for your business, and your profits.

Okay, the glaring fallacy with the argument is still that horseowners tend to have more than one horse.

Let's take a close look at California's figures, since California has plenty of horses and plenty of people.

Orange County, when it had two million people, had an estimated 21,000 to 35,000 horses. This equates to one horse for every 95 or 57 people--take your choice. I prefer the latter for a very simple reason--money, which in this case carries the label, "taxes." Yes, horses in some California counties are subject to personal property taxes, and profits from horses are taxed. Also, give consideration to zoning regulations. If a person has three horses, and lives in an area zoned for two, you can be pretty sure no one is talking the extra boarder. It is estimated, by virtue of recounts, that the Orange County horse population figure is low by at least 15 per cent. I don't think a lot of people want to tell the local tax collector just how many horses they own.

Alpine County only had 200 horses, but it also had only 1,100 people. That's one horse for every five and one-half residents!

Riverside County had 72,000 horses at the time these statistics were gathered--a horse for every nine residents.

Los Angeles is a big city of more than seven million people. Because it is a major metropolitan area, you'd expect there would be very little room for horses, and you'd be correct. You'd also be correct, as well as shrewd, if you figured that limited space for horses could be turned into a profit. (If you were thinking that before I mentioned it, the horse business will make you a lot of money, fast.) In Los Angeles, there are a number of people getting very wealthy because they saw the opportunities in housing some of the city's more than 130,000 horses.

That's a lot of horses for a city--one horse for every 55 persons. That's a whole lot of opportunity to make money.

Interesting, and not so surprising (if you are beginning to catch on) is the fact that Los Angeles' ratio of horses to people is pretty close to the national figure estimated earlier--one horse for every 50 persons.

All of the statistics so far relate to horse ownership. While only one in 50 persons in the U.S. may be involved with a horse, that certainly doesn't mean the other 49 aren't interested in horses. There are dozens of interesting horse activities, any one of which spells profit. Nearly 170,000 people go to the horse races every day. There are those who say it is the betting which draws the crowds. Betting, of course, does attract a number of people, but it is not THE attraction. Horses bring people. The proof is the fact it is now possible to bet on horses legally, in nearly every state where there is parimutual racing, without attending the races. If people want to bet on horses without ever seeing the horses, they can do so. But a lot don't; they still go to the track.

The fact people want to see horses race can lead directly to you making money with horses.

Someone has to breed, raise, train and care for all those horses at the race tracks around the country. Someone is making money doing those things, and that someone could be you.

People love horses and most would love to own one, or a share in one, or be involved in some way with one. And once a person becomes involved with a horse, it quickly changes to horses! If you now have a horse, or have had one, you know the truth of that statement. Horseowners are constantly buying, selling or trading, and somehow the number of horses a horse person has multiplies.

If you're not yet fully convinced of the opportunity for you to make a lot of money with horses, give consideration to this thought: less than one person of every two is without a car, yet the auto industry, even in bad times, is a constantly-growing sales opportunity. The market is limited, but the sales go on and on and on. More and more people are making a living in the car industry and its supporting industries.

What a fantastic market you have in horses! More than 40 of every 50 people in the U.S. are potential customers. And then there is the gigantic market of support industries--feeds, health-care, tack, information, education, competition. You could choose to be involved in any part of it. Finally, there is the world market, and the world's population is growing, and so is the world's involvement with horses. Hey, the Internet makes the world market part of your market in seconds. Don't ignore the new opportunities offered by technology.

Now that you have an overview of the market and the potential for profit, the next step to making money with horses is to get started.

Earlier I suggested you would have to choose to do the thing you like doing best. Your choices within the horse industry--if you want personal contact--are trading horses, racing horses, breeding horses, or training horses for various forms of recreation or competition, all of which involve the buying and and selling of horses.

Let me repeat now so there is no mistake. You will be involved in the buying and **SELLING** of horses.

Selling is the key to profit, for there are only two ways to make money directly with horses--win prize money or sell the horse. (Of course, there is plenty of money to be made selling services or merchandise to horseowners.)

Take your choice.

Choose what you love most. If you love what you are doing, you will succeed.

With your choice made, you now have to commit yourself to making a profit, or in other words, conducting business.

I won't waste your time with a lot of business advice. You can easily and quickly check on business regulations for your city, county and state.

You should need no help with securing a business license, resale number, or choosing your stationery. There are hundreds of good books and courses detailing how you can start your own business.

What I do want to give you are rules for the horse business which you must obey if you want to make money. These rules apply to every type of horse business because each type involves the same principles.

    1.   Concentration is the key to economic results, a truth you must recognize.

You will not be financially successful while engaging in many facets of the horse industry at the same time. Choose one area and stick to it.

    2. Knowledge is money in your bank account, and it will take study, study, and more study to just learn most of what there is to know about a single aspect of the horse industry.

There are more than 200 colleges and universities throughout the U.S. now offering degree programs in equine science. In addition there are noncredit horse courses available in nearly every city through community colleges. (You can even earn a college certificate of recognition taking my online course, Training Performance Horses, and never leave your ranch. For more online horse courses, see www.donblazer.com)

One of the riches to be gained in the horse business is lifestyle. The owning, promoting and breeding of a stallion is quite a different life from being the trainer of hunters, endurance horses or western horses. Pinhooking, the purchase of horses at one sale and resale of horses at another sale, requires a much different temperament than that possessed by the successful person who is racing horses.

Choose wisely the area in which you wish to concentrate your efforts.

Don't be fooled by the idea that work is drudgery. If horses are going to make you money, then you must do what you really want to do, which is enjoy yourself while you earn a living.

Choose to make money by applying your special talents in the activities easiest for you. If you are good at conditioning young horses, you'll want to be a trainer. If you love the study of bloodlines and the challenge of genetics, you'll like being a breeder. If your talents lie in dealing with people, you will want to be a trader or a syndicator.

Success is easy; failure is hard. Choose easy, and success is yours.

3. Over-expansion and under-capitalization kill or cripple thousands of businesses each year. Start your horse business on a scale you can handle financially. One horse can make you a millionaire, and 50 horses can make you a pauper.

If you choose to make the buying and selling of weanlings your business, one or two can make you thousands of dollars. You don't need 20 horses to start. What you need to start is knowledge and experience. If you make a mistake on the purchase of the first two, you can recoup and gain on the next three. But if you are financially overextend initially, disaster awaits.

If you intend to train horses, don't start by purchasing a training stable. Start by getting your first paying customer.

4. Since all business involves the buying and selling of a product or service, you must accept the fact that all profits lie outside your office, or home, or ranch. You buy and sell horses at sales, or on the Internet, or when meeting strangers, or when attending horse industry functions. You will not sell many horses by simply standing in front of the barn holding a "horses for sale" sign.

Believe it or not, horse trainers who are making a lot of money are not sitting on a horse all day. Wealthy horse trainers are in the show ring, at sales, at the races, or attending meetings of local horsemen's associations. Horse trainers who make a lot of money have horses they promote constantly before crowds of people. Horse trainers who are barely paying the rent may have trained a world champion, but you can bet no one knows about the horse.

If you want to get it (money), you have to flaunt it (potential).

5. Cut your losses! Never, never hang on trying to change a sure money loser into a money maker. Miracles do happen, but not often enough to make a profit. Once you have even the slightest hint a horse you are involved with is a loser, get rid of him immediately!

Which leads us to some other rules you must follow.

A. Always take a profit. You will make money taking a profit--even a small one. Lots of small profits add up fast.

B. You cannot keep a horse for sentimental reasons. For you, horses are not a hobby. If you want horses to make money for you, choose goldfish as your hobby.

If you want a friend, buy a dog.

If you think you can violate one or more of these rules, stop reading, and try to resell this book to a friend who wants to make money with horses.

If you are still reading, swear a personal oath to abide by the rules, and the profits will come galloping in.

You can achieve anything you can conceive. So you can have anything you want, but you can't have everything you want.

Chapter two
Know exactly what you are buying

There are many breeds of horses. As reported earlier, there are at least 142 active breed registries in the United States. The fact that there are so many breeds increases your chances of making money with the breed you like best. All the competition isn't concentrating on the same dollar.

If you are already committed to a certain breed, fine. Stick to it. That breed can undoubtedly make you a great deal of money, and richer still in other ways. The price of Arabians once soared as if by magic. Maybe it was. It is not the same today, but there is still plenty of profit in Arabians. Morgans are on a popularity roll. Peruvian Paso imports and resale prices staggered the imagination a few years ago. Trakehners and warmbloods (imports of almost any kind) are very hot.

Opportunities abound!

Select any breed, and by following the advice outlined for most facets of the horse business under consideration, you'll make plenty of money.

However, it would be nearly impossible to gather and compile recent statistics for each breed, since the data is overwhelming. Therefore, for the purposes of this book, and because I follow my own good advice (go where the money and information are most plentiful), I will use race horse (Quarter Horse and Thoroughbred) statistics most often. This doesn't mean there aren't other racing horses. Standardbreds are a very big business indeed. Appaloosas are running, and so are Paints, Arabians and mules. **And this does not mean this book pertains only to race horses. You choose the breed; the rules for making money with horses remain the same.**

But as much as you might like a non-racing or other breed, and as much as you might wish it weren't true, it is true--the greatest flow of cash is in Thoroughbreds and Quarter Horses. These two breeds command huge prices as race horses. In addition, they are extremely popular as show horses, trail horses and sport horses.

I deal in Thoroughbreds and Quarter Horses because I like lots of money, and I like it fast, and I like it easy!

The greatest number of public and private sales are for Thoroughbreds and Quarter Horses. The largest racing purses are for Thoroughbreds and Quarter Horses. The biggest prizes are for jumpers, cutting horses, reining and western pleasure futurity horses, all dominated by Thoroughbreds and Quarter Horses.

A word to the wise. Horses can make you a lot of money, and always a lot faster when you ride them among the high rollers and free spenders. **(No matter what breed or facet of the business you choose, never think cheap! The money is there, ask for it.)**

I said you must choose the breed you like best. So don't despair. If you choose to stick with any breed other than a Thoroughbred or Quarter Horse, the game--except for racing--is the same.

There is plenty of money to be made buying and selling weanlings of any breed. There is money to be made owning and standing a stallion of any breed. There is money to be made owning and breeding broodmares of any breed. There is money to be made training horses of any breed. There are riches to be made trading all breeds.

The information offered in the following chapters is as applicable to one breed as it is to another. So stick with what you like best; you'll be happier, therefore, eventually richer.

From this point forward, the statistics, the figures, the dollar amounts, the samples all pertain to Thoroughbreds or Quarter Horses because they are the easiest statistics to gather and the easiest to verify. (As I told you before, there are no made up examples in this book; you can check the accuracy of the figures if you've a mind to.) As long as the discussion is not about racing, you need simply make a mental conversion from Thoroughbreds and Quarter Horses to the breed you've chosen.

Inevitably **ALL** facets of the horse business, just as all other businesses, involve **BUYING** and **SELLING.**

Before you can buy and sell horses wisely, you must fully understand that **POTENTIAL** is the only thing which makes a horse valuable. The potential to make money by winning purses, the potential joy of winning horse shows, or simply the potential for pleasure found in owning a horse; that is what buyers buy.

Absolute nothing other than potential is important if horses are going to make you money.

Once you have decided to concentrate your efforts on a particular breed, you will want to become knowledgeable about the bloodlines, events, activities and sales associated with that breed. You must know what is "hot" and what is "not" within the breed industry. You must know the factors which create "potential."

After the horse's "eye-appeal", the most important tool for recognizing a horse's potential to make money is **THE CATALOG.**

Every registered or purebred horse, even if he is standing in a backyard in some out-of-the-way place, has a "catalog page." The catalog page reports all the facts about the horse's family and accomplishments in a particular way. It is your responsibility to understand the meaning, the sizzle, the weaknesses and the strengths indicated by the information on that page. You, and you alone, must assess the page and make the final decision on the horse's potential to make you money. The people who make money can read "money" in the catalog page.

The more you know about a catalog page and the more information on that page, the better the chances your decision will be profitable.

If you are buying a horse from a private party, and no catalog page is offered, it is your responsibility to contact the breed registry and dig out the needed information, then construct your own catalog page for appraisal and later sales material. Do not buy until you have constructed a catalog page. In some cases, an offered catalog page may only be a sentence or two about the horse's training or talents. That is not enough. Only by knowing all about the horse's pedigree can you determine all the potential areas for profit. And don't trust a catalog page which can't be verified. You can't verify the statement: "a sound gelding which will make anyone a wonderful trail horse." What you want to see is a list of accomplishments--such as--won the All Around Championship, Western World Show, 2002.

Before you buy any horse as part of your business, construct a catalog page so you know exactly what potential you are purchasing.

If you don't construct a catalog page for every horse you purchase, you'll be missing opportunities to make sales, which means missed opportunities to make money. If you don't construct a catalog page for every horse you buy or own, don't blame me for your losses. **It takes time, but you must develop a catalog page for every horse you buy and every horse you plan to sell.**

While there is nothing wrong with buying a horse from a ranch or breeding farm, there is usually a greater margin for profit when purchasing the horse through a sale. For one thing, it is much less costly to you to have a number of horses to choose from in a central location. Second, you have no personal expense in constructing a catalog page. Third, you must be more astute when buying privately, since you are relying entirely on your own knowledge and judgment. Most owners and breeders overestimate the value of their horses, and consequently ask more for them than they would bring at a sale. At a sale, you also have the consensus of opinion to back up your appraisal, and that is a major plus. Seldom will 20 or more other professional horsemen overbid a horse. When the bidding stops, that's about what the horse is worth.

Approximately 20 per cent of the foals born each year, as well as many older horses, are sold at auction through sales sponsored by private parties, racing associations, breeder associations, individual breeders, show organizers or companies exclusively in the horse sale business.

While horses purchased in sales do not necessarily perform any better than those not in sales, you do have advantages by purchasing at auction.

Many of the sales are "select." Select sales require the horses being offered to have been inspected for conformation and/or to meet some established criteria before acceptance. There are special sales for all breeds and for various performance talents. In the case of some yearling sales, the term "select" is almost a guarantee you won't get a bad horse. But it is also practically a guarantee you will have to pay an inflated price. Why do "select" sales create higher prices? Because the term "select" says "more potential," and potential is what buyers buy.

Don't be afraid of the price of a horse with potential. A high-priced horse with potential will resell at a still higher price, and a greater profit for you.

For the best profit margins, it is best to buy at sales and sell privately.

Catalogs are usually available several weeks prior to the sale date. You should obtain your catalog and study it thoroughly. Estimate the selling price of each horse listed, mark it on the catalog page, and then compare it to the actual selling price.

Good buyers don't miss by much. Making a good buy is as important, maybe more so, than making a good sale.

Studying the catalog carefully will facilitate your inspection of the horses which interest you. In most cases, the horses will be on the sale grounds a day or two in advance. In any case, you'll have a chance to see the horses hours before they go into the auction ring.

You should have each horse that appeals to you brought from his stall, walked away from you and back to you, turned and trotted. Determine for yourself if the horse is lame or travels sound. Ask the handler all the questions you have concerning the horse's health, training, disposition, and his behavior since arriving at the sale. Don't believe much of what you are told, but ask! It is too late for questions after the hammer falls. It is also surprising how much you can learn from idle chatter; listen carefully.

And give careful consideration to what you are not told. Most handlers will have a difficult time lying to you, but remember, they are usually quite good at not telling the complete story.

If it is a performance horse sale, make sure you attend the demonstration session.

An auctioneer will often let a horse sell well below its true value, but smart buyers--and there will be plenty--will seldom let a horse sell way above its potential for profit.

Buying correctly at sales requires experience.

You have to be attentive. Many items on the catalog page may have been corrected, added to or deleted. It is your responsibility to get the "updates."

You should know when to start bidding on the horse you want and when to stop. Don't be the first to bid; let other establish the early lower offers. And stop bidding when the bidding reaches your estimated/acceptable price. You can't pay the full price of the horse's potential as you see it, or there won't be room for your profit margin. You should study how some buyers "shut out" another bidder, and you should learn to catch sellers "running up" bidders. Consignors often bid on their own horses and quite frequently buy them back. Don't overpay by being caught in the excitement trap, or by allowing your desire to get started now overshadow your business sense.

Many sales will have a medication list. This reports all medications given to any horse in the sale. Be sure you check the list to see if horses you are interested in have been given medication. If the sale does not have such a list, check the "conditions of sale" in the front of the catalog to see what rights you have in case you discover a horse you have purchased has been given a medication.

Attend some sales just for practice before you actually start buying and selling.

The sample catalog page which follows is typical of the form used in major sales. Catalogs prepared in the manner shown instantly give you an idea of the quality of the horse offered. Some catalog pages are much more difficult to read due to their organization.

Naturally, the wording in the sale catalog is contrived to present the best picture of the horse's pedigree and performance record. Understanding what is not mentioned in the catalog, and learning to read between the lines will result in a even greater competitive edge than simply reading what is shown.

You absolutely must understand what the omissions mean.

The catalog normally starts with a title page offering the date and place of the sale. Several pages follow which list the conditions of the sale, officials, a map of the sale location and barns, a credit application, an agent authorization form, consignors, sires, dams, reference sires, applicable state laws, and other pertinent information particular to that sale.

Horses to be sold are listed one to a page. To insure fairness in positioning a horse in the catalog, most sales maintain a certain order, changing each year or each sale. Fasig-Tipton, one of the nation's largest sales companies, lists the horses alphabetically by the dam's name, each year starting with a different letter of the alphabet.

The sample catalog page lists a Timeto Thinkrich yearling.

(1) The Hip No. refers to the horse's position of selling. Number 17 means that this horse was to sell in the 17th position. But don't count on it. If you go out for coffee while the 14th hip is selling, you may find you've missed Hip 17 because Hip 15 and Hip 16 were scratched or "outs" (taken out of the sale).

(2) The owner, consignor, or agent.

(3) The name of the horse, if named, and the color, sex, and birth date. If a name has been asked for, but not yet approved, the statement, "Applied For" will appear instead of the name. When a name has not been applied for, the color and sex will be moved up above the birth date and the horse will be identified as "Brown Colt."

1 Hip No. **2** Property of

17

3 Gothinkrich

Brown colt; foaled 1979

Hip No.

17

4 Gothinkrich
1,463,937

	Timeto Thinkrich 99SI 996,508	Aforethought TB	{ Intentionally { Aspidistra
		Chronometer AA	{ Tiny Charger TAAA { Rhoda Watch AAA
	Chic Pat Go 102SI 708,142	Go Clabber AAA	{ Go Man Go TAAA { Clabber Tiny AAA
		Miss Bar Chick	{ Rocket Bar TB { Lucky V Chick

5 By TIMETO THINKRICH 99SI (1971). Champion 2 and 3-year-old colt, champion aged stallion. Stakes winner of 15 races, $612,858, All-American Futurity, etc. Sire of many ROM winners, including THE FORTUNE HUNTER 101SI (6 wins to 3, 1980, $175,232, Moon Deck S., 3rd Golden State Futurity, etc.), DENIM N DIAMONDS 96SI (6 wins to 3, 1980, Kansas Futurity Con. 2), Rich And Precious 99SI (at 2, 1979, 2nd Boise Futurity, etc.).

6 1st dam
CHIC PAT GO 102SI, 1970, by Go Clabber. 23 wins, 2 to 8, $123,729, Bay Meadows Abe Kemp, Miss Peninsula, 2nd Los Alamitos Salton Sea, etc. This is her first foal.

7 2nd dam
MISS BAR CHICK AAA, by Rocket Bar TB. 2 wins, $2,721. Dam of 8 foals to race, 6 winners, including—
CHIC PAT GO 102SI. Stakes winner, above.
Miss Vi Go 110SI (Go Clabber). 6 wins to 5, 1980, $16,286.
Moon Chic Go 87SI (Trish's Moon). 4 wins, $7,638.
Miss Banducci 86SI (Go Clabber). 2 wins, $6,349.
Go Bar Exspence 84SI (Go Clabber). Winner to 3, 1980, $2,815.

8 3rd dam
LUCKY V CHICK, by Triple Chick. Winner, $1,233. Dam of 5 other foals, 4 to race, including—
ANDY GO 99SI. 24 wins to 10, 1979, $111,054, HQHRA Champ, Mt.
|| Palomar, 2nd 49'er, Los Alamitos Catalina, etc.
Idaho Go 93SI. 15 wins to 9, 1979, $27,891.
Chic Bar Go. Placed. ROM producer.

9 4th dam
CLABBER'S LUCKY V, by Clabber. Placed. Dam of—
SCOOP BAM AAA. 7 wins, $8,674, Las Vegas S., 2nd Los Alamitos Champ., 3rd Shue Fly. Dam of 7 ROM, including—
SCOOPER CHICK TAAA. 13 wins, $60,642, Los Alamitos Hard
| Twist, etc. AQHA Champion. Stakes sire.
THREE SCOOPS TAAA. 6 wins, $14,506, Bay Meadows Belmont, 2nd PCQHRA Cal Bred Futurity. Dam of Scoops Alabai 95SI (4 wins, $23,323).
Scoopetta Chick 94SI. Winner, 3rd Santa Cruz Futurity. Dam of EASY SCOOP 94SI (5 wins, Arizona QHBA Lassie S.), Mighty Mayor 98SI (winner, 2nd Laddies S.), etc.
MINE KING 94SI. 8 wins, $8,155, Blue Ribbon Downs Cherokee S.

10 Engagements: Skoal-Dash For Cash Futurity.

(4) The name of the colt repeated along with the registry number, and the pedigree of the horse for three generations. In pedigrees, the sire is always listed on top, the dam beneath. The registry number of the sire and dam will also be listed, unless one is a Thoroughbred, in which case "TB" will be stated. The American Quarter Horse Association has a complicated system of registration. Sometimes an owner neglects to apply for registration, which may cause complications when buying from a private party. But in a sale you can be sure the horse would not have been accepted if the registration was not in order. In the case of unnamed foals, or older "appendix" horses, no registration number will appear.

If an asterisk appears in the pedigree, it means the horse was foreign bred.

Along with the registration system goes a grading system. Most breed associations award points or titles to competitive horses. For Quarter Horses there may be some combination of "A's", or awards, such as Register of Merit (ROM), or speed index (S.I.). Such designations will immediately follow the names of horses earning ratings or special awards.

In discussions of pedigrees, there are certain rules which must be followed. A foal is always "by" a sire, and "out of" a mare, never the reverse. Dams, granddams, great-granddams, always refer to mares in direct descent through the female. They always appear on the bottom line of each generation, thus sometimes referred to as the "bottom line", or more correctly, the "tail-female".

The top line of each generation, on the mother's side, is referred to as the "tail-male".

Numerical ordering is reserved for successive female sides, the tail-female. Thus the "first dam" is the horse's mother. The "second dam" is the grandmother (the dam's mother), and the "third dam" is the great-grandmother (the second dam's mother).

While the sire's mother is also the horse's grandmother, she is never called that; instead, she is the "sire's dam".

It is common to hear a horseman say, "This colt is by Timeto Thinkrich, out of Chic Pat Go, by Go Clabber." Thus your attention is always drawn to the female side of the pedigree. Seldom does a novice investigate the dam of the sire of a prospective purchase. Such investigation should always be made as it can be extremely revealing as to potential, that all-important concept for making money.

(5) A brief summary of the sire's racing accomplishments, his foaling date, and his performance at stud. Note that this summary is in bold face type. A great deal more information is desirable and available about the sire than can be contained in one paragraph, but you will have to research it yourself, and you should.

You should be well enough versed in your chosen field to know which sires produce high-priced offspring and which do not. You should know the stud fee of the sire, and have a good idea of the annual average selling price of his yearling colts and fillies. You should be aware of performance ability and the disposition of the sire's offspring.

Remember, the sire, if older, may have sired many good foals, but with limited space, it is nearly impossible to give more than a short report on his performance at stud.

The mare most likely will not have a produce record of more than 10 foals, so her entire record can be reported.

You will constantly hear the expression "black type". It is an extremely important part of buying potential. There are two rules. A stakes winner's name will be capitalized in bold face (very black) type. A stakes placed horse's name will be in bold face type, but not capitals. If you are purchasing horses other than race bred horses, the produce record of the bottom line remains just as important. Mares which produce outstanding performers in any field have great profit potential, and so do their offspring. The foals, if good, will have awards and accomplishments as important as black type.

Even though the sire's paragraph record is short, much can be deduced. The principle of listing the best first is followed. The line "stakes winner of 15 races, $615,858, All American Futurity," etc. tells much more than it says. You can conclude he won more than one stakes race, but only one of major importance, or it would also have been listed. At the time of this sale, The Fortune Hunter was his best foal, and his victory in the Moon Deck Stakes and his third place finish in the Golden State Futurity carried more importance than did the Kansas Futurity Consolation placing of Denim N Diamonds. (Of course, Denim N Diamonds later became a World Champion and a much more important offspring to Timeto Thinkrich. The future held more profit potential for Gothinkrich.)

(6) The first dam starts the summary of the "tail-female" or "bottom line", giving the birth date

so you will know the mare's age. The dam's name will be listed in capitals, but in light face type unless she is a stakes winner or stakes placed. If the latter, then it will be lower case letters, but bold face, or "black type". In this case, the first dam is a stakes winner, so her name is listed in both capitals and bold face. Her sire's name is listed, then the number of races she won, the number of years she raced, that is from two-years-old to eight-years-old, and the amount of money she won. You can tell she won only two stakes, because two are listed, then a second place finish in a stakes is reported. If she had won more than two stakes, all would have been listed. The second place finish would have been dropped if space for stakes wins was needed.

The catalog then states the horse being offered for sale is this mare's first foal. This is important, for not only must all foals be accounted for, but you must also account for all foal-bearing years. If a mare has many barren years, you want to know why. In this case we know she raced until she was eight (1978), so the mathematics work out. This is the first possible year that under normal circumstances, she could have a yearling.

A word about the race comment following the mare's name. If she raced, the record will be given. If she was unraced, it will say so. Only if the mare raced and was unplaced will no comment be made. This is virtually true of non-racing horses also. If a mare has performed even fairly well, the catalog will list even minor awards. If the mare has not distinguished herself in any field, there will be no comment. Another case of the un-said providing needed decision-making information.

The catalog shows Chic Pat Go has lots of potential.

(7) The second dam offers the highlights of the female family, but not all the details. Miss Bar Chick, as you can see immediately, has not won or placed in a stakes event because her name is in light face type.

Money won is also important, but no matter how much she won--it could be in the hundreds of thousands--she could not earn "black type". In this case, she had two wins, but only earned $2,721. This tells you her races were not quality races, the purses being under $3,000. Purse distribution varies at each race track, but the winner normally gets about 55 per cent of the purse. Miss Bar Chick was not running for much money, and her races were won at weak racing locations. You do know she earned a Triple A rating, and that is a minor plus in terms of her value. With non-racing horses, you must know what events are considered high quality and what awards create potential for the prospective purchase.

The next comment is tricky. "Dam of eight foals to race, six winners..." The catalog does not tell you how many foals she had, or why they didn't get to the races. But it does tell you she had more than eight foals, and that for sure she had two which did race, but couldn't win. Furthermore, as only five foals are listed, the sixth one to race definitely wasn't much.

You should also know the value potential of stakes races or the importance of other competition.

A weak stakes win or a victory at a very small show doesn't carry much value potential. Any other accomplishment which does have dollar value will be listed, even if the event is relatively small.

(8) The third dam, Lucky V. Chick, is reported to have produced five other foals, four to race. The five other foals reported do not include Gothinkrich's second dam, Miss Bar Chick.

The catalog only lists three of Lucky V Chick's foals. Of course, some omissions are necessary due to limited space, but in this case, Chic Bar Go never won, yet is still listed. Consequently, you can be sure the unlisted foal was worse than Chic Bar Go.

Sometimes after a mare's name and record, the statement "producer" will be made. This means the mare had produced at least one winner. It always means just that, no more, no less.

(9) Fourth dam. If a catalog includes the fourth and fifth dams, then it is an indication the previous dams were not outstanding. Or it may mean the fourth and fifth dams were exceptional, as in this sample. Then too, the fourth and fifth dams are older and have had more time to produce good foals. Here, the first dam has had only one foal, so extra space is available for the fourth dam, which has produced lots of black type.

You must weigh all the factors in deciding why a fourth or fifth dam has been included. Personally, I prefer so much black type or listing of awards and achievements in the first three dams that there is no room for the fourth dam. What is "up close," meaning the "immediate family", is what has profit potential.

(10) Here the catalog entries will change according to whether the horse to be sold is a mare, a horse, a weanling or a yearling.

A yearling, and in some cases a weanling, will have "engagements" listed, telling you to which important races or shows (futurities) the nomination fees have been paid. Engagements are usually indicators of profit potential.

A broodmare will have a race record, a produce record, and if she has a foal by her side, the foal's birth date and sire's name. Finally, if the mare has been bred, a pregnancy status is reported. The words, "believed to be in foal" are no guarantee the mare is in foal. If you are buying potential for profit, have the mare pregnancy tested prior to purchase at your own expense. The breeding date and the sire to which the mare has been bred should be listed.

If the mare was not bred, the catalog should state, "not bred," or "open."

In the case of two-year-olds or older, the training status or race status should be given, such as "unraced", "placed twice in four starts", "galloped 45 days". Comments for horses not intended for racing might include "halter prospect", "finished in top 10 at first show", "loads well", or "prospective jumper".

With horses, there is a special terminology applied to relatives.

Because a sire can have so many offspring, while a mare has only one foal a year, horses are never referred to as half-brothers, or half-sisters unless they are out of the same mare, but by different sires.

If the horses are by the same sire and out of the same mare, then they are full brothers, brother and sister, or full sisters.

A foal by the same sire, but out of a different mare, is never a half brother or sister, but is called a foal "by the same sire."

A final comment about the catalog page you construct or are given. Black type, awards, and permanent record achievements never become less than shown, but can constantly be added to by members of the family.

Hip No. 17 is by a young sire, out of a young mare. (Always potential, as nothing bad has been proven.) Both have the potential to add more and better black type or awards to their records. (The sire certainly did.) This may make Gothinkrich more valuable to some extent at a later date if he remains a colt. (More sales sizzle.) And similarly, his good performance will positively increase his dam's value and the value of her subsequent foals.

Chapter three
Weanlings: big potential for profits

At first glance, selecting a weanling of any breed seems to be the biggest gamble of all.

It is not! In fact, it may be your safest return on investment opportunity.

On the surface, you are dealing with a baby from three to 11 months old, unbroke except to lead and groom, and essentially untrained. And it is difficult to know exactly what you will have in a year or more. All this tends to make a lot of people stay away from weanlings, which means their price, at sales, is usually less than their true value. (Consider the fact that most weanlings sold at public auction will bring only about the cost of the breeding fee. Someone other than you paid to have the mare bred, paid to keep her for the gestation period of 11 months and 10 days, and paid to keep both the mare and the foal until sale time. Add to all that expense the normal health care costs, and it is easy to see a healthy weanling at the price of a breeding fee is a steal.)

So immediately you know you have two factors to your advantage. First, no matter what weanling you purchase, you know that in most cases you won't overpay if the price is about the same as the stallion's service fee. Second, most of the buyers at a sale are not interested in weanlings, so it is easier for you to acquire your top selection.

There are a lot of risks between the date of breeding and the time a horse begins to perform, whether it is racing, cutting, jumping, or driving. With the purchase of a weanling, you are splitting the cost of taking a horse to the point of performance. The price you pay for the weanling is the reward the seller gets for assuming the risks from breeding to weaning. If the seller doesn't make a profit, that's his problem. He probably didn't know how to have horses make money for him. If you buy a bargain, for you it is another step to a big percentage return on a small initial investment.

When you sell your purchase, you will get the reward for assuming the risks from weaning to point of sale. And those risks can be minor since the horse is generally under no major stress.

At the time of reselling--with no effort on your part--you have two more factors which are working to your advantage.

First, yearlings and horses ready to perform almost always bring the highest sale prices. (The exceptions are the elite stallions and mares just ready to begin breeding, and stallion or mare syndications.) Secondly, the high rollers are willing to pay an extra bonus for yearlings and horses ready to perform because they are eager to get started; they want action now, and they want your horse!

If you buy a healthy, sound weanling at a sale, and you care for it until it is a yearling, or is ready to perform, you will undoubtedly make a profit of some sort if you sell prior to the time the horse enters any form of competition.

You may have to tell someone you have the horse for sale, but sometimes, even that isn't necessary. I have purchased weanlings and resold them at a profit in less than three hours. (It has happened more than once when other buyers realized what a bargain I had purchased. I took a small profit--large percentage--and they still got what they wanted at a very reasonable price.) Weanlings are very salable.

However, you are in the business of having horses make you a lot of money, so you won't purchase a weanling just on surface appeal. You will be doing a great deal of studying. That means you will read every page of the sale catalog and you will compare every weanling offered with every other weanling. You will be looking for potential. (If you are looking for potential in weanlings not at a public auction, then you will have to construct your own catalog page. Develop the catalog page well in advance of looking at the weanlings. You can develop your catalog page by getting the name of the sire and the dam from the seller, then contacting the breed association for pedigree information.)

The purchase of a weanling, as the purchase of any other horse intended to make a profit, is based on potential and no other factors.

To reduce the risks of a weanling purchase even further, most horsemen, including myself, recommend buying fillies. If a colt can't run, win at the big shows, cut cattle, or jump, then both your resale and stud service potential are gone. Not just reduced, but gone!

You might get lucky and sell the colt (probably now a gelding) for a private pleasure horse, but you can be sure you won't get much.

Your possible resale buyers know the risks inherent with a colt, and so they are not anxious to spend the big bucks on anything less than a stallion prospect with superior bloodlines. Even a great-looking colt without an impeccable pedigree is a risk the majority of buyers at sales don't want to take. On the other hand, if a filly can't run, jump, or win the big shows, she can almost always produce foals. (You don't want her as a broodmare, because she most likely won't make you a lot of money, but that's covered in another chapter.) But because she can produce foals, someone will buy her. Older mares without a record still average a better resale price at sales than do older geldings or stallions without a record.

That's taking a negative look at some good reasons for buying a filly. But looking at the positive side, the picture is much brighter. Fillies generally bring higher prices at time of resale. Colts with weak pedigrees, whether weanlings, yearlings, or two-year-olds, do not command good prices. A colt with an average pedigree will bring less than a filly with an average pedigree. Fillies and mares maintain a higher average sale price at public sales than do stallions and geldings. (At "performance sales--the best performers, regardless of gender, bring the biggest prices. They are the ones with "potential.") The only time colts demand more than fillies is when the colts are extremely well-bred, good-looking and have big potential as a performer; then they are most often the sale toppers.

Of course, there is always the private sale, when almost anything can happen, and usually does. There is no ceiling on the price of fillies or colts at private sales. Colts do just as well as fillies at private sale, as you will note in an upcoming example.

The first example (see opposite page) is an unnamed bay filly by the stallion, Call Me Gotta.

This filly, foaled on February 13, 1981, has an excellent catalog sheet, and just about everything you would want in a pedigree to make a good profit. She has potential.

Call Me Gotta was a good race horse with solid bloodlines. As the catalog sheet shows, he was a Champion two-year-old, stakes winner and earner of $135,000. At the date of the sale, his first foals are yearlings, so there are no facts about his ability to produce, just **POTENTIAL.**

The first dam is Hula Skirt, a stakes winning daughter of Tru Tru. Hula Skirt only had an 87 Speed Index, and it would be best if you could purchase the offspring of a Triple A (AAA) rather than just a Double A (AA) mare. But, had she been Triple A, the price of her first foal probably would have been much higher, and that would not be good for you.

The weanling filly offered is the first foal of Hula Skirt, so she has no proven produce record, only **POTENTIAL.**

The second dam, Dancing Jacket, is a Thoroughbred, without a speed index. She was a winner, but not of much. This will keep the price of the weanling down slightly. What will increase the weanling's price, and her later resale price, is the fact that Dancing Jacket produced two stakes winners out of six foals. Four of the six foals earned their Register of Merit (ROM) and one of the six was too young at the time of the sale to have an established record; more potential.

Applied for

Bay filly; February 13, 1981

Applied for

Call Me Gotta 112SI 1.096.101	He's Gotta Go AAA	Go Man Go TAAA / Bavarian Bar
	Call Me Lady 95SI	Bar Depth TAAA / Call Me Now AA
Hula Skirt 87SI 1.481.536	Tru Tru 96SI	Truly Truckle TB / Gold Cupid AAA
	Dancing Jacket TB	Dancing Dervish / Elva's Jacket

By **CALL ME GOTTA** 112SI (1975). Champion 2-year-old colt, stakes winner of 9 races in 14 starts, $135,681, Sunland Park Futurity, RMQHA Derby, 3rd All American Futurity. His first foals are yearlings of 1981. Son of He's Gotta Go AAA, stakes-placed winner, 3rd Rainbow Derby Dash, sire of more than 80 race ROM, 5 stakes winners, including GOTTA GO CHOCOLATE 90SI ($83,394), GOTTA GO TOO 96SI ($75,480), BULLET BABY LADY 95SI.

1st dam
HULA SKIRT 87SI, 1976, by Tru Tru. Winner at 2, $9,195, San Mateo Invitational. This is her first foal.

2nd dam
DANCING JACKET TB, by Dancing Dervish. Winner at 2. Dam of 6 foals of racing age, including a 2-year-old of 1981, 4 ROM—
   MOVING DANCER 101SI (Smooth Move). 16 wins to 6, 1981, Boise 440 Champ., 2nd Boise 440 Champ.
   HULA SKIRT 87SI. Stakes winner, above.
   Lady Dancealot 85SI (Sir Winsalot). Winner to 3, 1981, $3,168.
   Skip Dancer 80SI (Skip's Request). Placed at 2.

3rd dam
ELVA'S JACKET, by Curandero. Winner at 2. Dam of—
   Dancing Duzy TB. 8 wins, 3 to 7, $14,470.
   Ajax Straw TB. 4 wins at 2 and 3.
   Parrandera AAA. 4 wins.

4th dam
LADY JACKET, by Bolero. 6 wins at 2 and 3, $15,955. Dam of—
   SOUTHSIDE MISS. 11 wins, 2 to 6, $75,021, Miss Florida H. Dam of 5 winners, including—
      Fire on Three. 16 wins, 2 to 6, 1981, $102,943, 2nd Florida Breeders' Futurity, 3rd Rough'n Tumble S., etc.
      Miss Morningstar. Winner at 2. Dam of **BRENT'S STAR** (4 wins at 3, 1980, $88,095, Beulah Kindergarten S., Heritage S., etc.), Gem Proof (4 wins at 2, 1980, $16,302), etc.
   Bed Jacket. Winner. Dam of—
      Like the Dickens. 12 wins, 3 to 6, $42,972.
      Camisole. 12 wins, 4 to 8.
   Centuple. 5 wins, 2 to 5, $11,700.
   Second Cabin. 5 wins, 3 to 7.

Registered Cal-Bred 27264.

The third dam did not do much, but the fourth dam was a winner and produced a stakes winner, and a stakes-placed mare Fire on Three, who ran out more than $100,000. Lake Jacket also produced another mare which was a winner and produced a stakes winner.

Note how well the female side of this breeding has done. The weanling considered is a filly. There is enough black type in the pedigree to guarantee more sizzle for the potential of the weanling being offered.

This is the kind of pedigree you seek; it is full of potential. It doesn't matter what breed you are purchasing. It is all the same--Paints, Arabians or National Show Horses--everyone is seeking a satisfaction and the horse you are looking for must have the potential to provide it. If the catalog sheet shows a lot of winners, at any event, then you've got potential for big profit in purchasing and reselling any weanling which interests you.

You are hunting for the catalog sheet which offers great potential. You are not looking at horses, you are looking at the potential they offer. You'll look at the horse later.

If the weanling is the daughter of a stakes winner who has produced stakes winners, the price of the weanling will probably be too high to make her a good purchase. Too much of a good thing will make it more difficult to produce a big return on investment without adding a positive performance record. And adding a postive performance record can be very difficulty. Once you go into competition, if the filly doesn't perform exceptionally well, then she will be a bigger profit loser. This is the case of a modestly-priced weanling being a better deal.

If the catalog sheets show no black type, no winners, no horses of merit, then even if the weanling goes for nothing, there is no potential for profit at a later sale. Skip very cheap horses. They are cheap because they have no potential and there is no way short of a miracle for them to attain the needed potential.

Hip No. 16 at the McGhan Sale sold for the amazingly low price of $8,000.

The filly was subsequently entered in the All American Select Yearling Sale at Ruidoso, New Mexico. As a yearling, being sold approximately 10 months after her purchase at the McGhan Sale, she brought $30,000, all based on potential.

The proforma chart on the filly shows a number of costs involved with her maintenance and subsequent resale. The cost of the weanling is a fact. California state sales tax is a fact. The veterinarian fees are an estimate. The estimated costs are, I believe, on the high side. This has been done to deliberately keep the return on investment at a modest rate. The return could easily be more than shown. For example, if you did not pay someone to take care of your yearling at the sale, then the expenses would be reduced by $300. A $300 reduction in expenses pushes the return on investment (ROI) up. I've estimated the cost of feeding and housing the filly for 10 months at $140 per month. I'm sure there are those who will say, "No way." But if you get your actual feed bills out and add them, you'll see it is easily possible.

In any case, even with the high estimated costs, the filly produced a profit of $16,620 in less than one year.

She produced a return on investment of 124 per cent.

CALL ME GOTTA Filly--Hip No. 16

	Expense	Income
Cost of weanling	$8,000	
California sales tax	480	
Veterinarian	380	
Farrier	100	
Pasture, 10 mos. @ $100 per	1,000	
Additional hay	200	
Grain and vitamins	200	
Transportation to sale	300	
Preparation at sale	300	
Futurity payment	500	
Cost of entering sale	500	
Selling price received		$30,000
Sales commission	1,500	
Total cost and expense	$13,380	$13,380

NET PROFIT...............$16,620

Return on Investment (ROI) 124 per cent.
(Total amount of profit divided by total investment.)
Now, if 124 per cent return on your investment in less than one year isn't a lot of money, I don't know what is.

Considering the initial dollar outlay was only $8,480, and the other expenses averaged only $440 per month, you have a small investment. But if you took the same total amount of money--$13,380--and put it in a treasury bill at the all-time high of 16 per cent, you would only have earned a profit of $2,140. A 16 per cent return on your investment would be considered an absolutely phenomenal return today, but it certainly won't make you as much money as a 124 per cent return. And if you put the money in a savings account at 2.5 per cent yield, the only absolute is that you will lose money. Inflation in 2002 was low at only 3 per cent. In a savings account there is no risk......you would have positively lost one-half per cent on your money in 2002. What interest rate are you getting today on your savings?

Also, keep in mind that you really didn't have a cash outlay of $1,500 of the $13,380 in costs. The $1,500 was a sales commission which was paid after the sale and prior to the time the $16,620 in profit was paid.

If you take off the $1,500, which did not come out of the seller's pocket, then the total out-of-pocket expense was only $11,880, making the monthly cost of maintenance an out-of-pocket expense of only $340 per month.

A ROI of 124 per cent on an $11,880 investment in less than one year sounds almost criminal. But it is a fact, and it happens, and it is easy to do again and again and again.

If $16,000 in profits is not big enough for you, then you'll want to go into business on a little larger scale. A word of caution--don't invest your lunch money. Know what you can afford to lose.

You can play the Make Money With Horses game on any level you like. It is up to you.

Here's what you can hope to do if you play with more dollars. These examples don't happen every day, but fortunately for us, they happen often enough not to be considered uncommon.

Majorie Cutlich purchased a weanling for $15,000. We don't know for sure what she spent in the next eight months to care for the weanling, but let's say she spent $10,000. That makes her investment $25,000. She sold the weanling after eight months for $270,000, giving her a profit of $245,000.

That kind of profit and return on investment ought to satisfy anyone.

But how about Donna Wormser who bought a weanling for $14,000? Let's say she also spent $10,000 keeping her horse for 10 months. She resold her $24,000 investment for $375,000 to make a net profit of $351,000 in less than one year.

If you think you can't make money--big money--in the horse business, think again.

Pinhooking is such big business now, that the major breed magazines include the activities of pinhookers as part of their report on horse sales.

When buyers are optimistic about the potential a horse offers, expect to see pinhookers making unbelievable returns. The last time I looked, pinhookers in the Thoroughbred industry were enjoying a very nice rate of return of 88.4 per cent. That was up from 56.8 per cent the year before. This is the age of opportunity for making money with horses.

Recent reports show weanlings costing less than $10,000 at the major Thoroughbred sales have resold for an average price of $40,000; that's a 148 per cent return on investment. Weanlings selling between $10 and $20,000 were returning 118.6 per cent. Now just so you will realize it is not all roses, weanling selling for between $30 and $40,000 returned only 16.9 per cent that year.

Here's another great return, except it is calculated on a very small budget.

This example is a colt. I don't recommend buying weanling colts for resale at sales, but they do make money. This colt was not resold at a sale, but was sold privately.

Nashville Shadow was purchased at a sale. His pedigree did not have as much potential as I would normally like, but it had some. The colt was an outstanding individual conformationally, which added substantially to his potential.

The first dam was a stakes-placed mare who had produced five foals to race. Three were winners, one of which was stakes placed. The mare, however, was an older mare--17 years old. She obviously hadn't produced as much as we would have liked, and it wasn't likely she would produce more.

What made me buy this weanling was the fact the mare had a very good-looking yearling colt which sold prior to the full brother weanling. When the yearling brought an excellent price, the weanling suddenly had a lot more POTENTIAL!

NASHVILLE SHADOW

	Expense	Income
Cost of weanling	$1,300	
California sales tax	78	

Veterinarian	300
Farrier	100
Board--$135/mo. for 7 mos.	945
All American nomination fee	50

Total cost and expense	$2,773	
Sold privately		$6,500
		2,773
NET PROFIT.....................		$3,727

Return on Investment (ROI) is 134 per cent.

Jet Charger had proven himself to be only a fair sire. He produced runners, but his potential--at 12 years of age--was limited.

Nashville Shadow was worth a risk only because he was a good-looking colt, his selling price was low--$1,300, the catalog sheet shows some black type and possibilities, and he had a yearling brother ready to go into race training, which could add some new sizzle to the potential. Still, this type of purchase should not be a high priority. It was a legitimate purchase by the rules, but not a great buy. The example is included only to demonstrate that weanlings frequently offer big rewards on small investments.

Nashville Shadow was entered in the All American Futurity, a million dollar race, to provide some sales appeal. The initial cost of entry was only $50, so the investment was minor in comparison to the "sizzle."

Nashville Shadow

Chestnut colt: April 11, 1980

Nashville Shadow
Appendix

	Jet Deck TAAA	Moon Deck AAA
		Miss Night Bar AAA
Jet Charger 101SI		Leo ROM
571.982	Rosa Leo AAA	Randle's Lady ROM
	Nashville	*Nasrullah
		Bonnie Beryl
Prattville TB		*Radiotherapy
	Paradio	Lucky Pay

By JET CHARGER 101SI (1968). Champion aged stallion, stakes winner of 14 races, $190.069, Texas Futurity, Raton Futurity, etc. Sire of over 90 ROM winners. including JET CHARGER 2 103SI (11 wins to 7, 1980. $75,574), PARTY'S JET 104SI (19 wins to 6, 1980, $41,497, Boise Derby, etc.). RIGADOON 98SI (13 wins, $26,964), START CHARGING 103SI (8 wins, $17,514), Rapid Rob 99SI (8 wins to 4, 1980, approx. $45,000).

1st dam
Prattville TB, 1963, by Nashville. Winner at 2. 2nd Paradise Valley S. Dam of 5 foals to race, including—
Kaweah Chris 85SI (g. by Alamitos Bar). 4 wins, $8,835, 3rd Parr Meadows Rocket Bar H.
Vilbo TB (c. by Hurry Ribot). 8 wins, 3 to 7, $17,393.
Butch Cassidy TB (c. by Hurry Ribot). 3 wins.
Santana Roo 88SI (g. by Quintana Roo). Placed.

2nd dam
PARADIO, by *Radiotheraphy. Winner at 2 and 4. Dam of 7 foals to race, 6 winners—
Prattville. Stakes-placed winner, above.
Glenwood Road (*Woodside View). 11 wins, 2 to 8, $31,546.
Parabo (Hurry Ribot). 4 wins, 3 to 5, $15,940.
Caldio (*Calstone). 3 wins at 3 and 5.
Sully Do (*Sullivan). Winner at 4. Producer.
Glenwood Lane (Unbelievable). Winner at 2. Dam of 5 winners.

3rd dam
LUCKY PAY, by American Smile. Winner at 2. Produced 5 winners, including—
Lucky Showers. 16 wins, 3 to 7. Dam of 3 winners, including—
Lucky Dawn. 4 wins at 3 and 4. Dam of 7 winners, including **Phoney Fran** (14 wins, 3 to 6, $21,575, 2nd Fashion H. at Longacres twice, Governor's Speed H. twice, A. E. Penney Memorial H., etc.).
Lucky's Wave. 7 wins, 3 to 7.
Pay's Echo. 2 wins at 3. Dam of winners **Sir Champ** (16 wins, $35,933), Tan 'em.

4th dam
PAJARERRA, by Luminist. Unraced. Dam of—
Shower Man. Winner.
Verde Ginger. Placed at 2. Dam of—
Bay Buz. 17 wins, 2nd President's H.

Eligible for Cal-Bred.

The colt was not advertised, but was shown to normal barn traffic. One such person liked the colt and purchased him for $6,500. The profit on the colt was $3,737 and the return on the investment was 134 per cent. Not bad for a horse held only seven months. Not bad, and yes, lucky. But you make your own luck.

When you consider the total investment was only $2,773, the profit was considerable.

The final example is included to show what happens when the rules are not followed.

Brides Request is a filly by a young stallion, A Zure Request. As shown by the catalog sheet, A Zure Request did very well as a race horse, and has the pedigree to be a good sire--that's potential, and it's what you're seeking.

The first dam, however, puts the purchaser of this filly in trouble. A Thoroughbred, Summer Bride was not a winner. She only placed at 3 and 4, which proves she wasn't a good race horse. There is no potential there.

As a producer, Summer Bride is the dam of four foals, three of which went to the races. Two foals were winners, and one of the two was a Quarter Horse, the same as Brides Request. That shows an ounce of potential. But even a pound of cure won't make up for the lack of "sizzle" come sale time.

The second dam, Dusty Bride, was not a winner, although she produced three winners. But do three winners add up to potential? In this case, no. None did much. And earnings of $13,456 for a Thoroughbred are very small.

Brides Request

Bay filly; May 8. 1980

		Azure Te TB	Nashville
			Blue One
Brides	Azure Request 108SI		Little Request TB
Request	1.158.285	Parr's Request TAAA	Miss Parr Charge AAA
Appendix		Summer Tan	*Heliopolis
X243.027			Miss Zibby
	Summer Bride TB	Dusty Bride	*Moondust II
			Kentucky Bride

By A ZURE REQUEST 108SI (1973). Stakes winner of 18 races,
$228,388, World's Championship Classic, Auld Lang Syne H.,
Horseman's QHRA Championship, Santa Clara Invitational H.,
Chicado Invitational H.. etc. His first foals are yearlings of 1980.
Son of AZURE TE TB, stakes winner of $119,630. among the
leading sires, sire of many stakes winners, including COME SIX
104SI, SIZZLE TE.

1st dam
SUMMER BRIDE TB, 1967, by Summer Tan. Placed at 3 and 4. Dam
of 4 foals of racing age. 3 to race—
Baby Be Sure (f. by Mazatl TB). 3 wins at 2 and 3.
Winter Groom (c. by David Cox QH). Winner in 2 starts at 2, 1980,
$1,730.
Summerofseventysix (David Cox QH). Placed to 3, 1979.

2nd dam
DUSTY BRIDE, by *Moondust II. Placed at 2. Dam of—
Broken Rudder (Hempen). 4 wins at 3, 5 and 7, $13,456.
Spa Prince (Hempen). Winner at 4 and 6, $12,252.
Gold Coin (Royal Coinage). Winner at 3 and 4.

3rd dam
KENTUCKY BRIDE, by Papa Redbird. Unraced. Dam of 12 foals, 10
to race, 8 winners, including—
Good Land. 8 wins, 2 to 6, $43,844.
Itty Bitty Bride. 4 wins at 3 and 5, $21,007.
Yellow Braids. Winner at 3, $3,751. Dam of—
‖ Vicam. 6 wns, 2 to 5 in France, 2nd Prix Achille-Fould.
Bridal Veil. Winner at 3. Dam of 1 foal to race—
‖ Idaline. Winner at 3, 4 and 5, 3rd Gus Fonner H.
Swoons Bride. Dam of **Bashful Bride** (to 4, 1980).

4th dam
MINSTRELETTE, by *Royal Minstrel. 6 wins at 2 and 4. Produced
10 foals, 7 to race, all winners, including—
JACK'S JILL. 17 wins, 2 to 6, $119,690, Hawthorne Gold Cup, etc.
‖ Dam of **OIL PAINTING** (13 wins, $124,775), **PATROL
WOMAN** (16 wins, $123,188). Granddam of **T. V. PRINCESS**
($129,033), **Clozon** ($56,782), **Quantum Jump, Clever Admi-
ral, Hip Hugger, Goer,** etc.
KY. COLONEL. 9 wins, 2 to 5, $64,097. Sheridan H., etc., Sire.
Balla's Girl. 8 wins, 2 to 5, 2nd Hawthorne Juvenile H.. Dam of
‖ CAMLOC (7 wins, $40,327). Granddam of **THREE
PIGEONS** (9 wins, $43,270), Cool Babu (dam of **HINDU
DIPLOMAT**, $88,816).
Firefly. Winner. Dam of **VENETIAN WAY** ($359,422, Kentucky
Derby, etc.), **HE'S A PISTOL** ($200,448, Breeders' Futurity,
etc.).
Eligible for Cal-Bred.

The third dam shows no potential either. And by the time you get to the fourth dam, even the black type there is too little, too late.

Brides Request sold for $2,000 as a weanling, and the cost of keeping her until sale time as a yearling were minimal. The total cost and expense was $5,495.

The selling price at the All American Sale was $6,500, and was predicated on the potential of the stallion, A Zure Request. (A Zure Request later proved himself the sire of some speed, and gained modest popularity.)

The net profit on the weanling filly was $1,005, and the ROI was 19 per cent.

Granted 19 per cent return on an investment of only $5,000 is pretty good in comparison with many other types of businesses. But it was somewhat risky because the total potential was weak. The potential of the stallion and the fact that the weanling was a filly--two of the rules to follow--are the only two things which saved this investment. Pass when the weanling offered doesn't show excellent potential on the catalog sheet.

BRIDES REQUEST

	Expense	Income
Cost of weanling	$2,000	
California sales tax	120	
Veterinarian	300	
Farrier	100	
Board @ $135/ mo. for 10 mos.	1,350	

Transportation to sale	300	
(Owner groomed and showed horse--no outside costs)		
All American Futurity payment	500	
Cost of entering sale	500	
Selling price		$6,500
Sales commission	325	
Total cost and expense	$5,495	
		$5,495

NET PROFIT.................$1,005

Return on investment (ROI) 19 per cent.

Weanlings are good profit makers, and often require a small investment and very little physical work. But you must follow the rules.

Rules for Pinhooking

1. Purchase fillies.
2. The weanling must be by a well-bred stallion who has proven himself a better than average performer, but does not yet have a long record as a sire.
3. The first dam must have proven herself an excellent performer, or an excellent producer. The produce of an average first dam should be passed.
4. The second dam must also be a performance winner, or the producer of performance winners. The second dam is still very important when seeking potential. She must show it. If the second dam is stronger than the first dam, that is even better. But a strong second dam can never

make up for a weak first dam. Do not fall into the trap of thinking you can slip one through and make a big profit based on a strong second dam. Smart buyers just won't pay the price, and the less than bright buyers only purchase cheap horses.

5. The third and fourth dams are not too important. A lack of black type or performance record will not hurt. Third and fourth dams, however, should have produced something. If they haven't produced, then the entire line lacks potential.

6. The weanling must be sound and without obvious injury when purchased, and when resold.

Potential is the key! The weanling being resold as a yearling will make money if she is good-looking, is by a solid, yet unproven sire, and is out of good-performing and/or producing first and second dams.

If you don't follow these rules, don't blame anyone but yourself if the weanling doesn't make money.

And if you say it's too hard to find weanlings which meet all the requirements, you are wrong. It's not too hard, it's just hard. That's one of the reasons buyers aren't making a lot of money with weanlings.

Pass the ones which don't measure up in conformation, blood, and potential. It is always better to pass 500 than to buy one bad one. If horses are going to make you a lot of money, then you'll have to put in a little effort and a lot of patience.

Don't buy because you are caught up in the excitement of the sale. Don't buy because you want some action. And don't buy hoping your normal good luck will make things turn out well.

If the dollar amounts in the examples are not big enough to suit you, just play with bigger bucks. (All breeds have the same potential for enormous returns on small investments.) You can play at any financial level. And you can play with more than one horse, so you can double, triple or quadruple your income anytime you choose.

The scale on which you decide to get started is completely up to you. The important thing is to get started. It is a business, and time is money, and you could be making a lot of it, now!

Chapter four
Yearlings (race or show) for sale

Yearlings provide two sure-fire ways to make money, and a third possible way to make a lot of money, quick.

First, if you buy yearlings for **immediate resale**, privately or at sales, you will almost always increase your bank account. I say almost always because there are those rare occasions when one gets sick or injured and the profits dwindle. Luckily, it is uncommon to lose money on a resale yearling, even if everything goes wrong. Generally, the profit just gets thin--but there is a profit.

Second, yearlings which are to be **shown, then resold**, are a greater risk; therefore they can produce a greater return on your investment. The problem, of course, is the greater the profit potential, the greater the chance there will be little or no profit.

A yearling to be shown, then resold, ties up your money for a long period of time, and may never prove the performer necessary to demand the big bucks. On the other hand, if the yearling turns out to be good--wow!

Third, there is the **yearling to race.** Here, the potential for return on investment is even better. So is the chance you'll lose money. But then it's only money and no guts, no glory. (Fortunately, it is not really as hard to make a profit as some may caution you. The tough part is following the guides--as it always is. I am confident, most of those who fail to make a profit violated one or more of the rules early in the game.)

Potential makes you money!

If you want to make money buying and reselling yearlings, then you must buy potential.

Potential can be anything, but you must decide in advance of any purchase what it will be and who will want to buy it from you.

That is rule number one.

If you are associated with people who want to purchase stock horses, then you must have a horse with a catalog page which proves his potential as a stock horse. If you plan to resell the horse as a jumper, the horse must be bred for jumping, have proven jumpers in his background, and have the potential to be at least 16 hands in size. (Don't ask me to explain the minimum 16-hand requirement. It is one of those notions which has no factual basis, but is part of the jumper industry. Silly, nonsense requirements are found in every segment of the horse world, as I'm about to tell you.)

By making a study of the market to which you will sell, you'll be able to identify a number of your own peculiar rules.

Since you are the one who will determine the potential in the yearling to resell, you are the one required to work hard to find a buyer seeking that potential.

In my case, I've made it easy on myself, again.

The potential I purchase is "flash". And the best "flash" I know of for a quick and very profitable resale is the color GRAY. (BLACK, however is quickly becoming a major color of choice.)

If the horse is gray, short, well-muscled, and not too clumsy, I'll sell him as a potential western horse. If the horse is gray, tall, Thoroughbred looking, I'll sell him as a potential English horse.

Silly? You bet. Make money? You bet.

No matter what else the horse is, if he isn't gray, I won't buy him or her for a resale yearling.

Now you are saying, "It can't be that simple."

Let me assure you, with the resale yearling, it is.

There just isn't any accounting for what a horse buyer will do. A future customer will tell you every detail about the horse he or she wants. But in the end, he or she will buy my gray horse--even if he is everything the customer didn't want. Don't waste your time and money trying to find the "exact" horse described by a customer. You'll lose money every time. Buy potential desired by the market you have chosen. The buyers are there.

All I ever sell in the resale-yearling is the potential flash of a gray horse. I never tell the customer the horse has the potential to do this or do that. I say, "This is a really nice gray horse." And then the customer tells me what potential he or she sees in the horse. I just agree. The buyer may never ask for gray, and the buyer may never actually realize that the color is what sold the horse, but that is all I have to sell, and that is what I sell. (Of course, I make a catalog page and show the page to possible customers. It is the customer who reads into the catalog page the potential he or she wants.)

I don't look for a sophisticated buyer. I don't attempt to sell the person on the idea the horse is a potential halter horse, or jumper, or dressage horse. I sell yearlings and two-year-olds to people who fall in love with the horse's color.

If rule number one is deciding the potential you will sell, then rule number two is: **never deviate from that potential.**

Suppose you decide you want to sell the potential of a halter horse. If you've put forth any effort at all, then you know something about the type of horse it takes to be a halter horse within the breed you've chosen, and in your part of the country. You know what your market wants to buy. If you haven't expended any effort to learn your market, then you'll need some luck and strict adherence to the other rules.

So you purchase a horse with the potential to be a halter horse. You've followed all the rules to this point; therefore, this horse has a catalog page to prove his potential as a halter horse. And of course, you have written out, or typed, the catalog page so you can show it to a customer, and so you won't forget to mention any of the horse's potential when you are presenting the horse for sale.

Have the catalog page with you at all times during the presentation. Do not violate rule number two by attempting to add anything to the horse's potential. Say only, "This horse has the potential of being a special halter horse." Point out the proof of potential on the catalog page, and then be quiet.

From that moment on, all you have to do is agree with the customer's own observations. If your customer wants to add to the potential of the horse by suggesting the horse has a wonderful disposition, or he might also pull a buggy, or that he sure looks as if he could barrel race, you just smile, nod your head and keep you mouth tightly closed. Don't you dare attempt to add anything more to the horse's potential; if you do, you'll probably lose the sale and the opportunity for a big, big profit.

You really don't know what the customer is looking for or likes other than he wants a halter horse. You have a potential halter horse for sale. You are asking a lot of money for the horse because he has such "great potential" as a halter horse. Anything else you may suggest will most likely be the wrong thing. I know, I've violated the rule.

Let the customer tell you what is good and what is bad about the horse.

If you don't violate rule two, you won't say the wrong thing, and then much sooner, rather than later, someone will purchase the potential you are offering, leaving you with a very nice return.

There are also some other guides, rather than rules, which can facilitate the resale of a yearling or short two-year-old.

Price the horse no less than three times more than you paid for it. If you purchased it for $1,000, ask no less than $3,000. A horse with the potential you are suggesting must be valuable, not cheap. You can always accept an offer.

Do not attempt to train the yearling which you plan to sell immediately. You do not want the horse to reach his potential. You want to sell the potential. You do not want to know how athletic the horse is, or what a pretty mover he is. What you don't know won't hurt you, and what no one knows is the horse's potential--the thing you are selling. In presenting the horse to the customer, do everything possible to make the horse as attractive as you can. Groom the resale yearling until he shines like a diamond. (You should never present a diamond in the rough. A customer may say he or she can see through the long hair and dirt, but neither can.)

Bathe the resale yearling with shampoos and coat conditioners. Make sure he sparkles. Blanket the resale yearling according to weather conditions so it is obvious to the customer that you recognize the potential of the horse.

And be sure the resale yearling is gentle. Any customer coming to view the horse's potential should be able to touch the horse, walk around the horse and rub his nose.

If you adhere to the rules and use the guides, resale yearlings and young horses should bring you profits as quickly and as large as the examples given in this chapter.

I purchased a gray yearling filly on the first evening of a five-day sale. On the second day of the sale, a gentleman approached me as I was longeing the filly in front of the shed row. He knew what I had paid for the filly ($3,000) and he asked if I'd be interested in a small profit.

Everything is for sale, I told him, and I asked what he would consider giving for my filly.

He replied, "Thirty-five hundred."

I handed him the lead shank and stuffed the cash in my pocket.

Now I didn't price the horse at three times what I paid for her, but then he knew what I had paid. I didn't suggest the filly was anything other than what he saw--gray. I accepted a 16.6 per cent return on my investment.

If you could deposit $3,000 in the bank, and get 16.6 per cent interest on your money at the end of one year you would consider it phenomenal. What do you consider a 16.6 per cent profit in one day?

By the way, I asked my buyer why he was so interested in my filly.

"My wife wanted a gray horse, and I want to get back to Dallas," he replied.

Don't think that this sale was one of those lucky once-in-a-lifetime things. I've done it many, many times since.

A friend recently followed the "know your market" rules and purchased "potential" in a sorrel filly. He paid $750 for the filly, and priced her at $3,000, more than three times what he had paid.

Aggressively talking to people in the market for the potential he had to sell, he resold the filly in less than 30 days at the price he wanted.

His expenses were $108.

His return on investment was 282 per cent. (Income, less cost and expenses, divided by the original investment.)

George makes his living by making two or three such deals a month, with an occasional gray thrown in for bonus bucks.

Resale yearlings can make you a lot of money if you purchase potential (which identifies your market), then resell that potential.

To do it, you must know and understand your market, go where the buyers are, or bring the buyers to your horse.

The second way to profit, the yearling or short two-year-old to be shown, then resold, requires you do enough training to demonstrate the potential you are offering.

If you can't do the training, or you don't want to do the training, then don't select this avenue as the road to your fortune. You will not turn a profit paying someone else to train a show horse. Trainers are making the profit if they are following the rules in a later chapter.

Potential for the young show horse must be identified, polished, and presented. Once named, you cannot change it. (It's a bad idea to change horses in midstream, and I know, I've made the mistake.)

I've selected the following example for two reasons. First, because I had a lot of problems moving this filly since she had a ringbone which discouraged many buyers. And second because this sale demonstrates what can be done if you add a little creative thinking to a rather simple plan.

I purchased a two-year-old filly at a sale. Her cost was $1,200. For my money, I got a flashy, extremely attractive, high-potential western pleasure horse with a high ringbone on the right pastern. Without the ringbone, she would have cost four times as much, which I never would have paid. (If I had been buying only potential I would have paid the price--she had the potential--but I buy facts too, and the fact was she had the ringbone. Therefore I wasn't willing to investment too much in a high risk situation.) I was willing to gamble on the ringbone because the filly had a great catalog page as a potential western pleasure horse.

I don't advocate that you buy horses with problems--they aren't the type of potential you want. But in this filly's case, she was not sore or lame, and I was confident I could keep her sound during training.

With the performance horse, as with all others, you are selling potential, never actualizing it. You must have a plan and a goal for the horse, which includes selling the horse long before you have to prove the horse's potential.

Take your time with the show horse's training, but don't waste any time in attempting to sell the horse. Start selling the minute you own the horse. Start training several days after you establish a specific plan and goal.

With this filly, her training progressed nicely, but her sale seemed almost impossible once buyers and veterinarians took a close look at the ringbone, even though she was never unsound. It surprised me a little. I always believe "management" of problems was part of the game. Apparently it is not for a lot of people, so a word to those who want to make money fast--don't buy 'obvious problems.'

If you have a problem, however, smile, manage it, and never get discouraged. There is always someone out there willing to pay for the potential you are offering.

In this case, it took a year to find someone willing to accept the risk, but not the entire risk.

I leased the filly. The lessee was to pay $250 per month in a lease payment, plus pay the filly's board and training each month. I was to be the trainer. I was to assume the cost of shoeing the filly and the cost of her health care.

The lease holder was happy because she was protected, could stop anytime, and would not be stuck with a lame horse. I was happy because the filly was now producing an income in two ways--being trained and being leased. I was sure I could keep her relatively sound as long as I was in control of her shoeing and her health care. In addition, I had some other advantages--someone else was doing my work, (showing the potential of this great western pleasure horse to possible buyers), and I still had the opportunity to sell the horse at anytime.

The lease was in effect for about a year before I sold the filly to a woman who had been trying to beat her at local schooling shows for more than six months. Since the woman couldn't defeat the filly with the horse she had, she decided to purchase a winner, and the potential for bigger and better things to come. (I never allowed the filly to be shown at a big show where she might be beaten.)

The venture produced the following financial result: I paid $1,200 for the filly and had expenses during the first year of $2,160 in board, $315 in shoeing and $200 in health care. The total investment at the time of the lease was $3,875.

I leased the filly for $250 per month, but still had $515 in expenses for the year during the lease.

The filly produced an income of $3,000 from the lease, and sold for $2,500 for a total income of $5,500. The total expense, including her original purchase price, was $4,390. The net profit was $1,110. (To show the worst, rather than best, the amount paid to me for one year to train the filly during the lease was not included as income attributable to the sale of the horse.)

The return on the investment (income less cost and expenses, divided by purchase price) was 92 per cent in two years, or 46 per cent per year.

If, as I do, you consider that a bad deal, then bad ain't too bad, and good is somewhere just ahead of fabulous.

The guide for making money with the young show horse is **never, never,** test the horse's potential. (I never allowed the filly to be shown except at schooling shows. The horse must always appear to any prospective buyer to have even greater potential than what they are seeing.)

Establish a performance goal, but sell before you reach it.

The young horse must be sold while he's on the improve, in training, still a potential champion.

The third money making method, yearlings purchased to race, then sell, requires more training, more time, more expense. The racing of a young horse is the riskiest of all methods by which horses can make money. It is also the single method by which you can become very wealthy overnight. I'm talking about a lot of money. And it has some tax ramifications which will be discussed later.

Everything is relative. Since you can get very rich running young horses, you must also be willing to carry some higher costs than normal, and resign yourself to having less involvement than normal.

You will also have to follow more rules.

I can cite numerous examples of people making thousands of dollars racing young horses. I can also point out examples of people who have made hundreds of thousands of dollars racing young horses.

Of course, for every positive example I offer, some guy will jump up and scream about all the people who have lost their shirts trying to race young horses. There's no doubt about it. Thousands of people have lost money with race horses. But the statistics aren't nearly as bad as some would have you believe. And you can bet the big losers didn't follow the rules.

The following figures are standard for the racing industry.

Only 2.58 per cent of foals ever win a stakes race. That's almost 50 to 1 odds against the foal succeeding and making you a millionaire. (What are the odds of something else (Lotto) making you a millionaire?)

Fifteen per cent of racing foals never perform. Twenty per cent race, but never win.

Twenty-five per cent win, but not enough to pay for themselves. Another 15 per cent win and pay for themselves, but do not warrant placement at stud or in the broodmare band.

Now here is the good news. Nearly 75 per cent of the young race horses don't make money, but **25 per cent do make money.** And the money they make is big money.

So you have one chance in four of hitting the big bucks. How full is the glass, not how empty?

And if you follow the rules, the chances are very good you won't lose much if you don't pick a money maker the first time.

First guide: hire a trainer who has a good earning percentage. (A high earning percentage means the trainer earns money--first through fifth--almost every time he races a horse. A good earning rate would be 50 per cent or above.) Total number of wins during a racing meet is not necessarily a good earning percentage. That means that often the leading trainer in total number of wins is not the trainer who has the best earning percentage. You want a trainer who sends horses out which earn money in nearly every race. And you want a trainer you can work with and trust. Do some investigative work, and talk with several of the best earning trainers before you make a final decision.

A cheap trainer is not a good trainer. If the trainer is cutting his or her prices, then some of the necessities for the horse are being cut. It can't work any other way.

Guide number two: don't change trainers if the horse isn't winning. Change horses.

There is no good financial reason for a good trainer to keep a horse which can't earn money. Only bad trainers keep horses which are losers. They want the owner to keep paying "day money."

A good trainer will tell you to get rid of the horse if the horse can't earn a profit. A bad trainer will tell you anything you want to hear, and keep presenting you with a bill. You'll soon be very far in debt.

Listen to the trainer and get rid of the losers. Cut your losses and let your profits run.

Guide number three: if your horse doesn't earn money within his first two races, find a new horse.

Guide number four: purchase a horse with potential, but not at a high price.

Remember the catalog page? You are the buyer now, not the seller. You are buying potential, but you don't want to pay for it.

Black type means the cost of the horse will sell high. That's not what you want. A lot of winners (but without black type) in the horse's background means the horse has the potential to run, but currently doesn't have the high-priced sizzle. That's what you want.

A few years ago, six of the top 20 money-earning two-year-old Quarter Horses were either traded or sold at auction. These horses all had the catalog of potential, but didn't command the high prices mistakenly associated with big money winners.

Tolltac was traded for approximately $5,700. He went on to win more than $1,000,000 and was later valued at $4 million by having a half-interest purchased at a price of $2 million.

Indigo Illusion was purchased as a yearling for $7,000. As a two-year-old, she earned $476,889. Face In The Crowd was purchased for $4,800 and earned $428,761 as a two-year-old. Drop of Moon sold for $8,200 as a yearling and earned $246,140 as a two-year-old. Double Dutch Bus sold for $14,000 and earned $219,654, while Rise N High was purchased for $6,500 and earned $210,000.

The other 14 top money earners were raced by their breeders, or sold at private treaty, but that's another chapter.

Guide number five: purchase young horses which are nominated to major futurities and derbies. Original nominations don't cost much, but offer potential and can't be replaced. Anyone can nominate almost any horse to a futurity or derby. If not nominated by a certain date, then there are penalties to pay for late entry, if late entry is even possible. Futurity and derby winning horses are not necessarily the fastest horses around, but they were nominated and are eligible to run.

If a horse is not nominated or supplemented to the race, it doesn't matter how fast he is; the horse can't win big money futurities or derbies if he isn't in them. The same, of course, applies to show horse futurities.

Guide number six: purchase horses bred in the state in which you race. State-bred races normally carry extra purse money. That means you earn more for doing the same amount of work.

Guide number seven: race your horse at the level at which he can win. It is not profitable to race a horse against competition he can't beat. No horse can make money for you if you refuse to let him earn. If someone claims your horse while he is winning, so much the better. You now have another chance to go for the million dollar winner.

The absolute rule of making money in racing: **win races and sell horses.** Having a horse claimed is the same as selling the horse.

Still skeptical about making money racing young horses?

Let me put it bluntly. It's risky. But one in four will earn money. That one could be yours.

In the meantime, so you won't be hurt financially, do the following things:

1. Sell any and every time there is a profit. You'll never lose money taking a profit.

2. Let your profit making horses run where they can continue to win and produce income.

3. Don't keep a horse that is losing money. Evaluate every three months. Lose money three months in a row, the horse has to go.

Now look around at those who are whining about having lost money on race horses. It's a certainty that they violated one or more of the rules and guides to profits.

Yearlings and early two-year-olds offer three sure ways to turn profits, but each method involves the eventual selling of the horse.

Some of the horses you own will turn out to be great show horses, some will be terrific race horses, and some will just be nice horses to be around. But, you can't keep them no matter how wonderful they are. If you want horses to make money for you, you must sell them when their potential is high.

Chapter five
Claiming to make a profit

If you think you can claim a race horse for $5,000 and move it up to a $20,000 race, or claim for $25,000 and move into allowance or stakes company, race horses won't make you any money.

Change your thinking. You are dreaming, not scheming. Dreams do come true, but not often enough to insure a comfortable living.

You've got to scheme--it's the only way to make money with claiming horses.

First, learn to think as a smart trainer, then claim cheap, race cheap and lose the horse cheap. The behavior of other trainers is what will make you money.

The statistics prove this premise, whether or not you wish to believe it.

You can make money only if you are cold, calculating and ruthless. You must steel yourself for a rough time, and you must be willing to try, try and try again.

Claiming horses are horses someone (trainers, maybe not the owners) wants to sell. By setting a claiming (selling) price on a horse, a trainer or owner establishes a level at which the horse supposedly can compete and win.

Most often the horses are worth less than their claiming price, which is an arbitrary figure used as a guide to bring horses into a race with other horses of equal ability and value. Frequently you can buy the horse at the barn for less than his established claiming price.

You can claim (buy) a horse in a race if you hold a valid owner's license, have a trainer and either have a permit to claim, or have a horse currently racing at the meet. Once you qualify, all you do is follow the rules by filling out a claiming slip completely and accurately, depositing the money (no personal checks) with the paymaster of purses and dropping the claim slip within the allotted time period. If the starting gate opens properly, and the horse you've claimed leaves the gate, he or she is yours from that moment on--win, lose, or draw, sore, sound, or broken down. If your claim is the only claim and is approved by the stewards, the horse is yours. If others have made a claim for the same horse, there will be a drawing immediately after the race among the claimants, and the winner will be given a pickup slip by the paddock judge. The paddock judge will also give a slip to the former trainer of the horse telling that trainer to deliver the horse to the new owner. Usually a claimed horse will be sent to the receiving barn for drug testing, and you, or your groom or your trainer, will pick the horse up there. Some tracks do not test all claimed horses and have specific areas where the horses are "haltered" by the new owners.

There are a number of other regulations about claiming, all but one of which can be disregarded at present. The regulation to keep in mind is that in many states, you are required to race your purchase during the next 30 days at a claiming price at least 25 per cent higher than that at which you claimed the horse. It's a move up the claiming ladder. It is what almost everyone wants to do.

Don't plan on doing it.

It's so hard to do, trainers call this "being in jail."

You may choose to run the horse at the higher price (example: if you claimed for $5,000, you must race during the next 30 days for a price of at least $6,250) just to learn about the horse, or to keep the horse fit without additional work outs. But running at a higher claiming price will be a learning experience only once. After that it will be a losing situation.

The horse may run well at the higher price, and even place. But it won't last, and it won't make you money. Instead of dreaming, believe the forthcoming statistics; they demonstrate vividly how the cards are stacked against you. However, they also contain the secret for success.

And keep in mind this is horse racing, and horses are the key. A horse which wins 25 per cent of the time for one trainer will most likely win 25 per cent of the time for you. A horse which only wins one race in 12 will probably only win one race in 12 for you. Horses are horses are horses, and no matter what trainers tell you about how good they are, the horses are the key.

Data gathered during a 99-day Quarter Horse meeting at Los Alamitos in California makes one fact very clear: claiming is not normally to the owner's advantage. It is a rating system used by trainers to establish a level for a horse and keep themselves in business. If a trainer claims a horse for someone else and the horse does well, that's fine. If the horse doesn't do well, the owner may get a tax deduction based on the losses.

Good claim or bad, the trainer gets paid his day fee, which is why, when asked about a poor performer in his barn, a trainer may reply, off the record, "He's better than an empty stall."

There were 242 claims made during the race meeting being used as an example. They were all recorded, including 19 horses which were claimed twice, and Miss Tripoli, which was claimed three times. Tracing all of them during the next six months was impossible, since some were sent to other tracks, retired, or used for purposes other than racing. Some of the ones which could be accounted for six months later are listed, showing their earnings since being claimed and their current claiming price. The sample (Chart A) is adequate to show trends.

The first pattern which develops from this history of claimers is that although some may run well at a higher claiming price for awhile, the majority tend to drift downward. In six months, 75 per cent are running at the same price, or lower than originally claimed. Of the 25 per cent still running for more than the original claim price, there is no guarantee they will earn money, will be claimed at the higher price, or could be sold for the higher price. Running at a higher price does not mean earning money.

The facts explode another myth--that certain trainers can locate a horse's problems, then improve him so he goes on to be a great champion. The record shows only three trainers actually showed a profit, and that modest, on their claims. Several consistently lost value with their claims, and none improved their new horses spectacularly.

Chart A lists 28 horses. If an owner paid a trainer an average of $1,000 per month to train, care for, shoe, medicate and race a horse, then the horses listed would have had to earn $6,000 just to break even during the six months following their claim. Only five of 28, or 18 per cent, did that.

Chart A
Partial listing of claims
242 claims, 28 listed, for 12.6% representation

Name	claim	since claimed earnings *shows profit	currently reentered
Kimala	5,000	3,000	8,000
Swiss Ban	3,000	3,000	3,000
Dos Rojos	10,000	2,200	6,250
Savan Dev	7,500	4,000	12,000
Bright Poli	3,000	500	Cl--3,000
Shake Kid	10,000	300	5,000
St. Blach	15,000	1,400	8,000
Beat The	4,000	1,000	3,200
Make A B	10,000	4,000	12,000
Pay the N	7,500	3,500	6,000
Hey Doc	5,000	1,400	4,000
Got the Ca	4,000	6,800*	12,000
Racin Fev	4,000	1,200	3,200
Lil Ranch	8,250	1,000	5,000
Fiery Com	5,000	5,200	5,000
Papa La Ru	12,500	10,000*	10,000
Mypawas	10,000	3,000	Alw

Wanyo	5,000	3,200	12,500

Name	claim	earnings	re-enter
Triumphant	10,000	6,700*	12,000
Bright Polic	3,000	4,200	3,200
Fair Brandy	5,000	2,700	8,000
Grove Line	7,500	10,000*	Cl-8,000
Shake Kid S	5,000	12,500*	8,000
Him a Injun	8,500	900	12,000
Pal and Pal	10,000	3,300	10,000
Sheckys Im	12,500	2,500	8,000
Diala Six	12,500	2,840	Alw
Star	8,250	4,400	12,500
Totals	211,000	104,740	222,350
Average	7,535	3,740	7,941

Analysis of Chart A reinforces the conclusion that claiming is a business for trainers.

(It is possible for you to become a trainer. It is not hard to do. Training race horses does not take a genius. If you want to make money with claimers, becoming a trainer to eliminate some of the daily expenses is worth consideration.)

The first trend (which is not shown) is that 82 per cent of the horses claimed were geldings. This is consistent with the fact that approximately 83 per cent of the horses in mixed claiming races are geldings. As geldings are good only for racing, this insures the trainer will have horses to train; they will not be taken away to the breeding farm.

While the five horses earning their keep did not earn a big profit, they didn't lose money. That's not bad. It's good. Because if the owners of other claimers had followed the rules, they very well may have earned profits also. In any case, the 18 per cent which made money demonstrates potential. You'll see how very soon.

Three trainers did make a profit on their claims. Interestingly, those trainers did not claim for an owner, but instead, claimed for themselves. At the very least, this would indicate when a trainer finds a good claim, he takes it for himself. For an owner, a trainer claims rather indiscriminately. (Remember, I said you had to be cold, calculating, and ruthless. I'll also give you another rule to live by when claiming--use the guides in this book, not the trainer's judgment.)

Now for potential.

Only two-year-olds have big potential. They have big money handicaps and stakes ahead. But there are few races with an inexpensive claiming tag for two-year-olds. Owners always tend to hope their horses will become the fastest on the grounds, even though the horses have proven they will not; therefore, since hope springs eternal, owners do not want to lose horses for a cheap claiming price.

However, when a maiden two-year-old is dropped to the bottom claiming price, has not had more than three races, shows at least one good speed index or some good works, he or she is a prospect to claim.

With only works to judge the horse, or less than four races, it is a pretty safe bet neither the owner, trainer, nor jockey has a true idea of the horse's future ability. In addition, a horse at the bottom as a two-year-old is not at the bottom as a three-year-old. (For race horses, the three-year-old year is the easiest, since they can run in races for 3-year-olds only and in restricted races: non-winners of two, non-winners since a certain date, fillies only, etc.)

Most two-year-olds tend to improve with practice and age. It is only the stars which win the first time out, or overcome minor mistakes to run an excellent race. Most good, solid horses develop as they go along. In addition, with only three or less races, the chances are fair the horse is still relatively sound. (Sore shins are most common problem and that can be managed.)

Two-year-olds with slow works, slow speed indexes, more than three races without a win and currently not racing against the very best, are not good claims if you intend to make money. Don't claim them.

Three-year-olds are a good claim only at the beginning of the year. Three-year-olds with less than six months of racing left are poor claims. Very soon they'll be racing with older horses, and that most often squeezes their earning potential. Don't claim from this category.

But, if you're interested in a three-year-old, it must have at least six months of racing left as well as meet all the other rules for claiming.

Older horses, four and up, seldom make money for an owner. They are a good claim to keep a trainer in business because they at least produce "day money". See Chart B. Only claim older horses which win at least 25 per cent of the time.

From Chart B, several interesting patterns emerge. The figures are accurate, while the patterns are logical conclusions drawn from those figures. (It is impossible to know the actual thoughts behind the claims.)

Twenty-nine trainers claimed 57 horses. Only 12 of the claims made money--21 per cent of the total. Four of the claims were for the trainers, so that reduces the owner's money-making percentage to only 14 per cent.

Chart B
Analysis of claims by trainer

Name	claimed	price	since earnings * profits	currently entered
Brittos	other	8,250	1,000	5,000
Campbell	" "	10,000	4,000	12,000
Cooper	" "	7,500	800	4,000
" "	" "	10,000	2,200	6,250
" "	" "	5,000	5,200	6,250
" "	" "	10,000	6,700*	12,000
" "	" "	15,000	9,000*	16,000
" "	" "	12,500	2,500	8,000
Domingu	" "	4,000	2,400	4,000
Francisco	self	3,000	4,200	3,200
" "	other	7,500	3,500	6,000
Frey	" "	4,000	1,200	3,200
Greenslat	" "	5,000	3,200	5,000
Hall	" "	5,000	2,200	6,000
" "	" "	5,000	4,800	10,000
Hart	" "	7,500	4,300	3,200
" "	" "	8,250	600	6,250
" "	" "	7,500	7,200*	16,000
" "	" "	8,250	4,400	5,000
" "	" "	7,500	11,400*	12,000
" "	" "	5,000	1,400	4,000

Halloway	" "	7,500	4,000	12,000
" "	" "	10,000	300	5,000
Holloway	other	12,500	1,400	8,000
Jackson	" "	3,000	3,000	3,000
' "	" "	5,000	500	5,000
Jones	" "	3,000	5,300	3,000
Lopez	self	12,500	10,000*	10,000
" "	" "	5,000	10,000*	8,000
Maldonat	other	15,000	4,700	12,500
" "	" "	10,000	8,200*	16,000
Olemach	" "	8,500	900	12,000
Pisciotta	" "	10,000	2,600	6,250
Proctor	self	3,000	5,200	5,000
Rothblu	other	7,500	10,000*	10,000
" "	" "	4,000	300	4,000
" "	" "	12,000	2,800	Mdn
Schvanev	" "	10,000	3,300	10,000
Steinmiller	" "	5,000	6,500*	4,000
" "	" "	4,000	3,100	4,000
" "	" "	6,250	3,700	10,000
" "	" "	4,000	1,000	3,000
Stokes	" "	3,000	2,400	5,000
Vischer	" "	5,000	2,200	5,000
" "	self	5,000	6,400*	6,250
Welch	other	3,500	4,600	4,000
Wells	" "	5,000	3,000	8,000
Walker	" "	5,000	3,800	4,000
Wimber	" "	3,000	500	3,000
Wenzel	self	4,000	6,800*	12,000
" "	" "	5,000	2,700	8,000
" "	" "	20,000	5,600	25,000
Woodho	other	10,000	3,000	stakes
" "	" "	8,250	2,800	6,250

" "	" "	15,000	11,700*	16,000
Wood	" "	8,500	600	12,000
" "	" "	8,500	2,800	12,000

Of the eight claims which made money for the owners, all were part of several claims made by that trainer. When all the claims for that trainer were combined, none showed an overall profit.

On the other hand, a claim made by a trainer for himself is practically risk free. The trainer doesn't have the high overhead of an owner. The claim provides the trainer with a horse to run, and as the trainer normally runs the horse one step below the original claim price, he stands to make a little money, even if he loses the horse.

Don't let Chart B give you the impression all trainers exercise poor judgment in claiming for owners, or that trainers don't know how to make good claims. What Chart B doesn't explain is that many of the claims were probably insisted upon by owners, even when the trainer recommended against the claim. Sometimes following a claim, owners refuse to allow the trainer to make money with the new horse because the owner won't let the horse run at the original claiming price or lower. Also, many claims are made to get the horse as a broodmare prospect. The horse may run again at a very high price with the prayer she'll increase her earnings a bit without the possibility of being taken. This is foolish, but is done quite often. Usually the mare could be purchased outright for less than the claiming price. And most often she doesn't make money at the higher claiming level.

Some claims lose money just on bad luck--injuries being the most common.

Study Chart B and you will see that Cooper claimed six horses which earned $26,000 in six months, less an estimated $36,000 in training expenses in six months, for a loss of $10,000 in the six month period. Trainer Hart claimed six horses earning $29,000, with a $7,000 loss.

Trainer Rothblum claimed three horses earning $13,000, but had a loss of $5,000 for the six months. Trainer Woodhouse made one good claim which pulled two bad claims up to the break-even. One other trainer broke even.

The losses and break-even for these claims for owners are based on the owner paying $1,000 per month in training expenses. So the earnings, less the expenses for six months, produce the loss.

Only one trainer, Lopez, shows a profit--and that is from horses he claimed for himself.

So how do all these negative factors show any potential for you to make money with claimers? Easy! The horses which make money for either owners or trainers follow patterns the statistics don't show. You must study the horse's form and take a personal look at the horses and their races in order to have the information you need to follow the rules to making money with claimers.

You cannot violate a single rule!

"That's tough," you say.

You bet it is. But not violating a single rule will make you money, while others who are violating the rules lose money.

Here are the rules:

1. Find performance consistency at a single claiming level (price). A horse which wins one in four for another trainer will most likely win one in four for you.

A horse to be claimed must be consistent, either in his works or his races. With two-year-olds, this is especially important since the horse will not have much form.

Consistency means the horse has earned money--first through fifth place--in no less than 75 per cent of his starts. Consistency can also be "on the board", meaning first, second, third, or fourth 50 per cent of the time.

No consistency, no claim.

2. A horse may be claimed at his consistency level, or one level below. He cannot be claimed above, or two levels below his consistent price.

As an example, if a horse has been running consistently on the board, or earning a check at the $6,250 claiming level, then he should only be claimed for $6,250 or $5,000. A drop below $5,000 means the trainer is trying to get rid of the horse, rather than just dropping to win. Trainers drop big to sell because they know there is always someone who thinks he can fix the horse and make him better. You know it can't be done, so let someone else lose money trying.

3. If you must run the horse within 30 days to keep him qualified to race, and you must move him up 25 per cent, then run the horse one step above his claimed price. After that, drop him back to the price at which he was claimed; or if you want to make more money, drop him one notch below his claimed price. If you are not required to "jump" the horse during the 30 days after claiming, run the horse back at the price for which you claimed him.

Keeping the horse at the price claimed makes all trainers think there is something wrong with the horse, and they usually won't touch him for at least two races. A drop one notch below the original claim almost assures you no one will take the horse until they've seen him run at least three times, even though he is probably winning.

If the horse was consistent at $6,250, for example, he'll do well at the $5,000 claiming level. He'll make you even more money if you race him for $4,000. And 99 times out of 100, he won't be claimed. If he is, you'll probably still make a good return on your investment just off the purse money he has earned.

For everyone else, the challenge of claiming is moving the horse up the claiming ladder. That's an ego trip. For you, claiming can be fun, but can't be about ego; it is a way to make money--so never move a horse above his consistency level. (If you get a super-horse and can move him up it will be very obvious, and the rule becomes "let your profits run.")

Someday, if you claim often enough, you'll get a horse which can move up dramatically. If you get one, move him up, and immediately start trying to sell him privately at an inflated price. You will be selling potential again. No horse stays up forever, and you must take a big profit whenever it is offered if you expect horses to make you money.

4. Never claim a maiden three-year-old.

Once in every 100 claims you hit a big winner, but most of the time you'll lose money. The only time you might risk taking a three-year-old maiden is if he or she has superior breeding and has been running with stakes company. Suddenly the horse is dropped into the claiming ranks, appears sound and is cheap. This horse may produce an income if no attempt is made to "move the horse up". Most likely the horse has a major problem of some kind, and will have a limited racing career. I say stay away from the horse. Taking a three-year-old maiden is just gambling and a violation of the rules. But on occasion, if all the factors add up to potential, and you don't mind losing the money, drop the claim slip. Just don't blame me. You gave in to temptation.

5. Claim only from trainers who are less than the best.

Good trainers get all the run a horse has to offer, so the horses are usually consistent. They should be consistent for you too, but often it will take time to figure out the horse, and while you are doing it, it is costing you money. Take horses from trainers who have large stables, or have poor in-the-money records. If you followed the rules, the horse you take will be a good one in spite of the trainer, and should be easy to keep going on a consistent money-making level.

6. Claim a horse which doesn't appear to be in top physical condition, but is still consistent.

Don't take a horse which needs running bandages to get through a race. Take a horse which has a poor hair coat, or even one which is under weight. You can't fix chipped bones or torn tendons, but you can easily and inexpensively fix teeth, deworm and feed adequately.

Even though you know you can improve the physical condition of the horse, continue to run at, or below, the original claiming price.

7. Never claim from the lowest claiming price offered at the racing meet. If the bottom claim is $3,000, the lowest claim you should make is $4,000. Once a horse is at the bottom, there is no place left to go. You cannot find an easier racing

level. The only exception to this rule applies to two-year-old maidens. The bottom for a two-year-old is usually at least two steps higher than it is for three-year-olds.

8. Never claim a horse you know has an injury.

9. You cannot move your horse to a higher claiming level until he has won for you at the claimed-for price at least twice.

If you claim a consistent $6,250 horse for $5,000, run the horse back for $5,000. If you are required to run at a 25 percent jump, then do it once, and get back to the $5,000 level, or even better, to the $4,000 level. This should assure you of at least a paycheck. (If you claim for $5,000, run for $4,000, win the purse, but lose the horse, you probably make no less than $1,000 profit considering the winner's share should be $2,000 or more.) If you don't win and don't lose the horse, any income helps cover training costs until the next race, which the horse will most likely win--if you have been following all the rules. Once the horse wins twice, you can jump him one claiming level. If the horse is getting paychecks, and is claimed on the first or second win, I guarantee you'll be making money.

Once the horse has won twice, move him up one level and keep him there for four races. He should win one in four. If he does, fine; if he doesn't, drop him to the original level. You can jump the horse again if he stays in the money consistently and wins twice again for you at that level.

Make no excuses for the horse's performance. If you run the horse five times at the claimed-for level and he doesn't earn money at least four times (sometimes bad racing luck is a fact--things happen, but are not an excuse), drop the horse one level and try him five more times. He should earn four out of five times, or he gets dropped. He cannot move up until he wins two races at that level. If there is no lower level at the track at which he is racing, find a weaker racing program and send the horse there.

These rules apply as long as the horse stays sound. If he has a physical problem, decisions will have to be made.

Getting sentimental about a race horse, or fearing he'll be claimed will cost you money. You cannot make money with a horse if he isn't earning.

Of all the ways to make money with horses, claiming is the toughest. But you can do it, if you don't violate the rules.

Your intentions and desires will be reality in your future.

Chapter six
Broodmares are risky profit makers

This chapter is rather short, very blunt, and included only because broodmares are a major segment of the horse industry.

I hope that introduction makes you think that I consider broodmares to be a very risky venture.

Good. I do.

However, broodmares admittedly can make you a lot of money.

But they probably won't.

At least the odds are they won't if you take the conventional approach.

If you have a mare, breed her, and sell the foal, you probably won't make a dime. In fact, the vast majority of the time, you'll lose money. That's a fact. Sure, I know all the stories about all the big breeding farms which sell yearlings for hundreds of thousands, even millions of dollars every year. And those stories are correct. However, that's exactly why you won't make money. You can't compete with the big farms, and it takes a big farm to run a conventional breeding program.

I'm fully aware that 99.44 per cent of the people in the horse business think broodmares are a gold mine. Well, some of them are, but unless you are already very wealthy, the chances are you'll never own the gold mine.

Great mares are worth a ton of money. And the return on investment can be phenomenal. But they are few and far between.

Miss Jelly Roll, dam of the Quarter Horse, Pie In The Sky, (winner of the All American Futurity and an outstanding sire) was virtually given away at an early age.

As the story goes, Miss Jelly Roll was sold as part of a package. Harriet Peckham wanted to buy a particular mare, and in order to get her, she had to take Miss Jelly Roll too. The price quoted was for two mares, and the seller would not change the price or the package.

Ms. Peckham decided the one mare was worth the full price, and Miss Jelly Roll could come along as a freebie.

After producing Pie In The Sky, Miss Jelly Roll was sold for a reported $1,000,000. Now that's making money with a broodmare.

But it's not the conventional approach.

The conventional approach is to breed Miss Jelly Roll and sell her foals.

At a cost of $1 million, Miss Jelly Roll would have had to produce at least five foals which would have sold for a minimum of $250,000 each at the age of one year before the owner would get close to breaking even, let alone making money. Now if do get five foals to sell as yearlings, it takes no less than seven years of maintenance, insurance, breeding fees, etc. And as of this writing, Miss Jelly Roll has not been a profit producer and never will be, in the conventional sense.

Most of the time in life we have to learn by experience. We touch something hot, it burns, and we know better the next time. Sometimes, as I have learned, you touch something hot a second time before you get the message. I've lost money on broodmares, not once, not twice, but several times.

Please, let a word to the wise (that's you) be sufficient. In the horse business, there are some truths which should not be ignored. No hoof, no horse, is one. Another is: you can't buy great broodmares, you have to make them.

No matter the breed, no matter the work, a mare must be proven in order to be considered great. Only great mares produce big profits for their owners, and owners don't sell the gold mine.

A mare can be proven in two ways. If she is to continue to bring profits, she must ultimately pass both tests.

First, she must perform. It doesn't matter whether she is a halter horse, pleasure horse, or race horse. She must perform and win.

Winning makes her valuable. It gives her the that important potential needed to be a producer. And remember, as always, it is the potential and nothing else which makes you money.

Her second test is as a producer. She must produce winners in her field if her potential is to remain strong and profitable. If she fails in either area, she fails as a profit maker for you.

Only a small percentage of mares are proven. The others are already losers, and will be failures as profit makers for the remainder of their lives. (There is always some mare, somewhere who proves the exception. But you won't make a living looking for exceptions.) Remember the catalog page you must develop? By now, you should know a bad catalog page means little profit potential for you.

If you've been in the horse business for one year, then you've heard someone, somewhere, say, "If she can't perform, we can always breed her." In early chapters I suggested people buy young fillies with that thought in mind, because it is that thought which will get your filly sold if she fails on potential. Someone, thankfully, will think they can breed her and make a profit on the babies. By the time you get done with this chapter, I hope you are not that silly.

Most mares don't achieve a winning record. Without a winning record, they don't have potential and can't produce profits for you.

The theory of selective breeding says: breed the best to the best to get the best. Everyone knows it's true, but most horseowners ignore it.

A mare may not show well nor race well, but still her owners go right ahead and try to breed her and sell the foals for a profit. But since she isn't a great mare by the first test--performance--she won't be approved for breeding by the owners of the best stallions, or her owner won't risk a high breeding fee.

So they breed a mare whose record indicates she should never be bred, and they usually breed her to something which should be a gelding. They then stand around and wonder why no one wants to buy the foal. (You wouldn't purchase such a horse because the catalog sheet would show no potential.)

If the owner attempts to show the offspring as a performance horse, the chances of success are slim and none. The expenses are going to be high, the training time is going to be long, and the offers to buy are going to be few. Less than the best, bred to less than the best, usually results in a less than the best performance horse.

The cycle is vicious and always a financial loser.

The rule: don't breed mares which don't have proven potential. They must be winners in their field.

If you can't accept this rule without more proof, examine the results from any recognized sale. Prove it for yourself by looking at the catalog sheet of every horse, and see, and believe, that the produce of mares without potential don't sell for enough to cover the cost of breeding and maintaining the mare, let alone the costs of raising the foal and the expense of selling at auction.

If that is not enough proof, go ahead and touch something hot. After the burn heals, read the remainder of the chapter.

If you can, sell any mare you have which does not have proven potential. You will lose money on her, but it is best to cut your losses now so you can invest in a mare with potential.

A mare with potential is a mare which has some kind of record. Either she was a winner herself at some endeavor, or she has produced winners.

If she hasn't done either of those things, you won't make money breeding her and selling the foals. Buyers know the rule of breeding the best to best to get the best. And you know it too.

Buyers will pay big money for obvious potential, and that is all they will pay for. They will not pay for the offspring of a mare which cannot win, or has not produced winners.

Check the results of any broodmare sale, and you will find well-bred mares without a record selling for $3,000 and less. Their foals will most often bring much less than the stallion service fee.

There are two ways to get mares with potential to make a profit.

You can make the mare yourself, by showing or racing her, or you can search for a bargain.

Making the mare yourself can cost a fortune, and often take years. If you enjoy showing or racing, and that is what you wish to do, fine. Just keep in mind that you are having a good time, and have chosen the long, hard road.

I hope it pays before you are too old to enjoy the final financial rewards.

Personally, I prefer the easy route. Find a bargain.

Finding a bargain doesn't require a lot of work, but it does take patience; as you've been told, all that glitters is not gold.

The bargain mare must have a minimum of two things going for her.

First, she must have a proven record as a winner. A good mare for profit must have national association points in some competition. If you've selected a particular breed, contact the association for information on awards. Make a catalog sheet.

In Quarter Horse racing, for example, a mare with high profit potential as a broodmare will have earned a Triple A rating or a speed index of 90 or better as a race horse. She will be a winner. At the very finest Quarter Horse sales, about one third of the horses for sale will have been produced by AAA mares. Since select sales are already supposed to be the cream of the crop, you can see AAA mares are few, and therefore in demand. They have potential.

Of course, you don't just buy top mares at bargain prices every day. You have to look for them, and when you find one, she must meet another requirement.

She must have at least two foals on the ground which are not yet old enough to have proven themselves.

You are seeking a profit, and you are selling potential. The two foals on the ground will do two things to help you make money.

Her two foals prove she can get in foal and carry to term. She has proven potential to produce more foals.

Secondly, those two foals are potential winners. And that is an idea you must expand upon if you want to make money with broodmares. You must use their potential as a selling tool to maximize your profit.

When you find a mare which meets the two requirements, and you can purchase her at a bargain price, you are in a position to make a profit with broodmares.

But if you are smart, you won't take the conventional route. You won't be selling the mare's foals to make a profit; **you are going to sell the mare**.

You are going to sell potential.

Keep in mind it was not Miss Jelly Roll's foals which sold for $1 million, it was Miss Jelly Roll.

It is not the produce of the good mare which will make you money, but her potential to produce.

Once you have a mare with potential, you have several approaches to profit.

You can work to resell the mare immediately for a gain.

This is the easiest and surest way to make a profit, and it only requires that you let the market know you have what it wants. You can advertise the mare in selected publications, or call directly on prospective buyers, or enter the mare in a public sale.

Double the original price of your mare, add in the costs of entering the sale and some padding for expenses while at the sale, (even if you don't go to a sale, that is the way to set a sale price) and with some sales effort on your part, a buyer will be happy to pay you handsomely. Remember, mares which pass the test are in demand, so you are in the driver's seat. Present the mare to possible buyers with confidence. Be sure you have your catalog sheet handy as your primary selling tool, and don't forget the potential of her yet unproven offspring.

If you want more than a 100 per cent return on your investment, get the mare in foal to the most popular stallion you can afford. Note: I did not say the best stallion available, I said, "the most popular".

Just about everyone in the horse industry thinks he or she knows about bloodlines and genetic crosses. Few do. Don't try to be a breeding genius. Go with the trend. You are breeding the mare to make money, not produce great foals. When a particular bloodline is hot, take advantage of it. Sell the market what it wants, rather than what you think is good; then you'll make money.

The most popular stallion in your market area should be easy to locate. He's the one producing the winners in the same field where your broodmare shows her potential.

You should be able to sell the mare in foal to a popular stallion easily for at least triple her original cost, plus expenses and the stallion service fee. Don't be afraid to ask a good price for the mare. If she has the potential, there is a buyer looking for her.

There are no buyers looking for cheap mares without potential.

Finally, you can take the risky, long-term approach and pray for big profits.

Breed the mare to the most popular stallion you can afford, and do it for the next several years, all the while hoping one or both of her first two foals prove they can win. If one of them does win big, you'll have to beat buyers away from your door.

If good fortune smiles on you (and that's the part I don't like about broodmares--waiting for good fortune to smile), you've got a money factory.

If pure luck misses you, then you can probably still get out with only a small loss if you sell the mare and her foals as quickly as possible. Once it is a fact the mare is not producing winners, her price will drop substantially.

Do not hold a mare longer than four years. If she hasn't produced a big winner from her first three foals, it won't matter much what she does later on. The horse industry is fickle and can't forgive failures. So even if the mare finally does produce, her value will be stifled by her earlier lackluster performers.

The only people I know making big profits breeding mares and selling foals are the extremely wealthy who can afford to breed the very best to the very best. And while they report their success stories, I'm positive none announce publicly the far greater number of losses.

A very unfortunate and unpleasant fact about broodmares and foals is that the fatality rate among young horses is extremely high. Sad, tragic stories are very common.

You can make money with a broodmare.

But the only sure way to enjoy profits is to sell the mare and her potential.

Forget selling her foals. As you should know by now from your study of sale catalogs and results, you can buy someone else's weanlings and yearlings cheaper than you can raise them.

And you've already learned how to make money with weanlings and yearlings.

Chapter seven
Stallion profits are in syndication

If you are willing to put up with the problems, do the selling work yourself and wait a few years, you can make money with a stallion.

If you get extremely lucky, you can become a millionaire in a couple of years.

But it probably won't happen the way you think.

The secret to making money with a stallion is to take the gamble out of the venture, and put hard work and salesmanship into the business.

But before I tell you the details of making money with a stallion, I want to explain why so many lose so much attempting to stand a stud.

Let's look at some probabilities and statistics which will demonstrate what you are up against if you take the conventional approach. This approach is to prove the horse good enough to be a stallion in selected competition, then stand him to outside mares and derive income from the breeding fees.

How tough and how costly is it to make a name for a prospective stallion? Well, if you've ever competed at halter, jumping, pleasure, reining or racing,   you know there are always more losers than there are winners. There is a lot of politicking which goes into the making of a champion, and a lot of advertising and a lot of traveling. Quickly estimate what it has cost you to race or show your horse in the past year. Is he one of the top horses in the nation competitively? If not, but you still think he has the ability, how much more in time and money do you think it will take?

My most conservative estimate is that it takes $30,000 per year to get a show horse national ranking. A race horse, on the other hand, is making money if he is nationally ranked. But then it probably cost no less than $100,000 to purchase the horse as a yearling, or to breed and raise him.

If you can get the horse national recognition for less, terrific!

Just to be nice, let's say your horse is nationally ranked by your breed association. Now what? Well, there's the competition to get mares.

The following figures are calculated guesstimates. There is no single source, no factual data on stallions at stud. I am using Quarter Horses as an example because the amount of public information is large and available, thereby giving the guesstimates a higher probability for accuracy.

It is estimated there are already 9,000 Quarter Horse stallions standing in the United States. No one knows for sure because no one counts. The majority are not publicized regionally or nationally, and a great many are simply standing in backyard operations. The same, I'm positive, is true with other breeds. So while the number of competing stallions may be much lower in the breed you have chosen, the total number of horses would also be lower.

Let's be generous again, and suggest all the stallions have good bloodlines, even though half or more are by and out of horses with no popular pedigree. Remember the catalog sheet? How good is the catalog sheet on stallions with which you are familiar? Probably not as good as some of the local competition.

Now let's be realistic and see what it is that attracts mare owners to a particular stallion.

It's potential!

To be successful, a stallion must show potential to produce winners. And he shows potential by having been a champion himself, or by having such an outstanding predigree--one absolutely loaded with winners--that everyone believes he can't help but produce.

By focusing our attention just on race horses, we can reduce the statistical numbers to a manageable level.

There are approximately 30,000 running Quarter Horses born each year. Nature being what it is, one half, or 15,000, are colts. Of these, at least 7,500 are gelded, die or are otherwise eliminated as stallion prospects. So there are about 7,500 prospective new sires each year. For simplicity's sake, assume as many older sires are retired or die, so the number remains constant, and competition doesn't get any tougher.

Only 2.8 per cent of all running horses ever win a stakes race or become a champion, meaning only 210 of the 7,500 possibles have attractive potential. If you are dealing with show horses, you are well aware the odds of producing a champion are just as tough, if not tougher.

If 15,000 of the 30,000 Quarter Horse foals are fillies, only about one-third (5,000) enter racing each year. Of the 5,000 we know attempt to race, only 20 per cent ever win any kind of a race, including cheap claimers. But let's say any winner is good enough to breed. That leaves 1,000 possible new broodmares.

The total each year is 1,000 qualified new broodmares for 210 qualified stallions.

That means there are less than five good mares for each good stallion.

Data from a regional West Coast Quarter Horse magazine reveals 195 stallions advertised, 62 of which were running horses. Of the 62, seven did not list a fee, or were advertised at "private treaty", meaning the fee was negotiable.

Fifty-five stallion breeding fees were listed, 38 at $1,000 or less and 17 at more than $1,000. The average breeding fee was $1,200, with the median fee being $850.

Using our earlier figures, a qualified stallion could expect to get five qualified mares per year, at the average breeding fee of $1,200.

The total income to the stallion owner would be $6,000 per year. (Don't consider mare care and boarding at this point.)

Not too good. Wait. It gets much worse.

Factor in $1,000 (very reasonable) to maintain the stallion for a year, and 12 advertisements at an average price of $670 each, and the outlay for those two items alone is $9,040. This represents a loss of $3,040. (Remember, this loss is for a horse that cost no less than $30,000 to qualify as a stallion prospect.)

You can't make money losing money that fast.

But you are positive you'll get more mares, so the breeding income will be much higher.

Good thought. Maybe you will. I hope so. If you check with the breed registries, you'll find most stallions are lucky to get five mares booked a year. And remember, if you get five good mares, any others are probably unqualified mares and will do more damage to your stallion's reputation than they'll ever return in dollars during the first few years. Once a stallion has foals on the ground, his potential for profit is gone. He must now earn points on results, and that is much harder to do. It is so hard, in fact, that the very best stallions in the nation, the cream of the crop, are considered to be doing well if they produce four or five good winners a year. And those super-studs aren't breeding just five good mares a year; they are breeding dozens. In addition, the top 20 stallions of any breed have been around for awhile. You won't knock them off the mountain with a new stallion, unless he's just been named "Horse of the Year."

By looking at the facts, the competition, the costs involved in qualifying a stallion, it's obvious you probably won't get rich taking the conventional approach.

However, a stallion can make you money if you maximize his potential and use your location to your advantage.

Syndication is your answer to big profits.

Let me show you how the big money does it, then show you how a little money can do it.

In a standard syndicate, there are usually 40 shares, so theoretically, in a $30 million dollar syndicate, each shareholder pays $750,000. If each shareholder is entitled to one breeding per season for 10 years, each breeding costs $75,000. This is pretty standard in the Thoroughbred industry. You would think then that the resulting foals from each breeding must earn or sell for at least $75,000, plus expenses, for the shareholder to break even.

But it is all done with mirrors!

Just suppose each investor put up $750,000 in cash and the syndicate buys the stallion for, say, $2 million cash.

Now the syndicate has a $2 million stallion--no slouch, and with plenty of potential--and $28,000,000 in cash. You can do a lot with that, and they do.

You have to have a place to stand the stallion, so the syndicate purchases a nice ranch for $4 million. They operate the ranch as a business, but breed to no outside mares and have no horse-related income. Operating expenses are projected at 400,000 per year, including depreciation on the stallion.

The interest alone on the cash remaining, if well-managed, will generate about $2 million a year above expenses, or $50,000 for each partner. So the foals really only cost $25,000 and still have the potential to earn or sell for much more than that amount. And they usually do. Research the sale prices of early Easy Jet and Secretariat foals--they sold for hundreds of thousands of dollars.

In the syndication chart, you'll see the partners will still make a profit even if the foals of the syndicated stallion return less than their actual cost.

Syndication
Capitalization (000 Omitted)

	Cash	Property	Total	1 Share
40 @ $750	$30,000	---------	$30,000	$ 750
Cost of stallion	(2,000)	$2,000	30,000	750
Cost of ranch	(4,000)	4,000	30,000	750
Operate 10 yrs.	(4,000)	-------	26,000	650
Depreciation	--------	(2,000)	24,000	600
10 % for 10 yrs.	20,000	--------	44,000	1,100

Net worth 10 yrs	$40,000	$4,000	$44,000	$1,100
Partner's return from 5 foals, net of expenses of $20,000 each				$100

Partner's value of 1 share plus minimal foal return $1,200

Percentage return on original investment, minimum expected: $1,200,000 equity less $750,000 original investment equals increase of $450,000 divided by $750,000, or a 60 per cent increase.

Pretty good deal. You get a 60 per cent increase in your investment, five foals, all of which could make a profit, and part ownership in a ranch which could be worth many times its original cost.

Okay, okay, you say $30 million is too much for you. You don't know anyone with $750,000 to invest, and you don't get invited to parties where the guests discuss buying and selling $2 million stallions.

The syndication doesn't have to be for $750,000 per share. Can you handle $2,500 per share?

You can! Well let's get started, because this is where you put in work and a bit of salesmanship. Then you reap the profits from syndication, not from the stallion.

First you have to find a suitable stallion prospect. This won't be a snap. It will take some searching and research, but you can do it.

Always keep in mind that the horse must have potential. His potential is in his record as a competitor and in his bloodline. Both must be much better than average. Find a stallion with a record you can sell.

Develop a catalog sheet you can use to show his potential in black and white.

Don't lose a good horse trying to shave the price. The price must fit the syndication, and you can pay up to $60,000. You'll get the cost of purchase back through depreciation.

Potential. That's the key. You must find the horse with potential you can believe in and get others to be excited about.

You know your horses and your market. Don't attempt to go national. Sell where you are located, so the horse becomes the local hero and dominates your local area. Local shareholders will also help you promote the horse. They want to profit, too.

Buy a horse you know your prospective shareholders want. Buy a horse with potential your prospective shareholders can see. Wins, victories, championships are easy to see. They are a permanent record.

Once you have found the horse, secure a purchase agreement and start selling shares. (There are lots of books on the market which provide detailed guidelines for syndication agreements, or an attorney can write an agreement for you.)

As with all the other methods of making money with horses, the profit is in the horse's potential and your ability to sell that potential.

Sell the shares, and without anything special happening during the next 10 years, there's a good possibility the percentage increase of each share will be close to 300 percent.

In the chart, I used a 10-year average breeding usefulness. Lots of stallions go on longer, but exhaustive studies by the Internal Revenue Service (IRS) have set this as a guideline for tax purposes.

At 40 mares per season, that comes to 400 breedings per sire. Some will argue the figure is too low, but not every breeding results in a live foal, and some years the horse's book may not be full. It's a good average and is used widely in the industry.

At an average service fee of $1,200 your stallion will earn $480,000 before expenses. Only in exceptional cases will this vary. I hope it will happen to you.

The stallion's bloodline will not change, nor will his competitive record, if he is retired to stud.

However, the performance of his foals could make a big, big difference. His first few foals should give you an idea of whether or not his fee must remain constant, or can be increased.

In part, it is up to you to do all you can to make his foals outstanding competitors. Don't leave it to chance or to someone else. Get out and promote the potential of those foals.

PROFORMA EARNINGS OF STALLION SYNDICATION

	Cash flow	Total equity	Share value	Percent increase
Investment $2,500 times 40 shares	$100,000	100,000	$2,500	-----
Purchase of stallion with record and potential	(60,000)	100,000	------	------
Expense of syndication	(1,500)	(1,500)	-------	------
Expense of stud lst year	(16,000)	(16,000)	------	------
Depreciation of stud straight line, 10 years	------	(6,000)	-------	------
Estimated income 15 mares at $1,200 per mare	18,000	18,000	------	-------
Income from excess cash	2,000	2,000	------	------
Status at end of first year	42,500	96,500	2,412	(3.5%)
Expenses, second year	(16,000)	(16,000)	------	------
Depreciation, second year	-------	(6,000)	------	------
Estimated income 35 mares at $1,200 per mare	42,000	42,000	--------	-----

	Cash flow	Total equity	Share value	Percent increase
Investment income, estimated at $40M	4,000	4,000	-------	-------

Status second year	72,500	120,500	3,012	20.0%

Expenses, third year through l0th year	(128,000)	(128,000)	--------	-------
Depreciation, third year through l0th year	--------	(48,000)	--------	-------
Estimated income, 40 mares for 10 yrs.	$348,000	$348,000	--------	-------
Investment income, estimated at $100M	80,000	80,000	--------	--------
Status at 10 years	$408,500	$408,500	$10,212	308.0%

Note 1. Average appreciation on investment, 30.8 per cent, per year.

Note 2. This performa is on an average stallion with no great achievements by his foals to increase his stud fee. It is assumed his foals were good enough to keep his book full.

One good son or daughter in the first, second, or third year, and your stallion's service fee could double or triple. More importantly, a good son or daughter creates demand for the stallion, and that creates demand for syndication shares at an increased price. Shares can be sold and resold.

In the proforma chart offered, I haven't allowed for any special luck. I've kept the service fee the same for 10 years, shown only 15 mares bred the first year, and only 35 mares bred the second year. You can do better than that if you work at it.

I've been conservative. You can be too, and still make a great return on your investment and efforts.

If you get very, very lucky, the sky is the limit. You could make millions.

But, you protest, "What if I don't get the number of mares projected each year?"

And I reply, "That could happen whether the horse is syndicated or not. And it probably will."

If you own and attempt to stand even a qualified stallion, the chances are good you won't get enough mares per year to make it pay. Very few stallions do.

If you don't think that is true, and you don't want to believe my earlier statistics, just open any equestrian magazine and pick out any stallion being advertised, even the top ones. Now multiply the breeding fee times 40 mares per year and that is his income. Subtract the cost of the stallion, his maintenance for a single year of his life, annual advertising, insurance, and a few thousand for incidentals and you'll see there is little or no profit.

Now figure the same stallion syndicated for $100,000 or $2,500 per share. If everything stays the same--costs and income--you'll be ahead by $40,000 or $50,000. That ain't hay.

It's not the stallion which makes money; it's his syndication, based on his potential.

Stallions can make money for you. But it won't usually be in the conventional way.

Syndicate and you will make money in the form of return on investment as a share holder.

Syndicate and you will make money as the general partner, through salary for services.

Syndicate and you will make money boarding and caring for the stallion ($16,000 per year in expenses, remember. That's in your pocket.)

And if you syndicate, you will make money from the revenue generated by mares brought to the farm for breeding.

Follow the rules. Syndicate, be willing to get out and sell the horse's potential, and have your shareholders sell their friends and neighbors, then wait a few years.

SYNDICATION OR LIMITED PARTNERSHIP GUIDELINES

How you go about establishing a syndication is up to you.

You can approach syndication several ways. You can be casual, writing a very simple agreement to be used strictly with friends and neighbors, without making a public offering. Or, you can make a public offering. In either case, you may wish to use the services of an attorney to prepare your partnership agreements.

The choices are up to you. I want to make it perfectly clear, I am not, nor is the publishing company, Success Is Easy, practicing law. I am not an attorney, nor am I your attorney. It is important you understand there are many legal ramifications to making any kind of public offering in which persons invest money.

WARNING: Shares in limited partnerships are considered securities under all state and federal laws. The offer for, and sale of securities, are regulated by law. If you want to prepare a limited partnership agreement, the following is a guideline only. It should be used only to offer ideas as to what you may wish to include and cover in the agreement. The following information is provided as suggestions only. Consult an attorney to create a Certificate of Limited Partnership, a document which must be filed in the state in which you are establishing the partnership.

A limited partnership, or syndication, usually consists of a general partner (in this case, that would be you) and several limited partners. You, as general partner, would have control over partnership affairs, and would make all the decisions concerning the partnership's business.

The general partner may or may not invest in the partnership.

The general partner--keep in mind this is you--has unlimited liability for all partnership debts and obligations.

The limited partners are not active in the day-to-day business activities of the partnership. They only invest money, and therefore their liability is limited to their investment. If the partnership is sued, creditors cannot attach the personal assets of limited partners. The partners are protected.

You can have a few limited partners, or up to 40, the number of shares you would expect to sell in a stallion. (The stallion will be expected to cover 40 mares per year--one for each partner.) A limited partner may buy any number of shares, so some partners may have two shares, while others could have 10 or more shares. The idea is to sell out the total number of shares planned to produce the total amount of venture capital needed.

You must keep complete records on all persons entering the partnership. List yourself as the general partner, and then list all the limited partners, including their residences, businesses and e-mail addresses, phone numbers and fax numbers. In addition, you will keep an updated record of the shares purchased. The partners are not required to give the business additional money if it is needed at a later date, but they can do so. Careful, accurate record keeping is a must.

Name the partnership. When syndicating stallions, the partnership is usually named after the stallion, such as, "Paint Me Profits" limited partnership.

You must name the principle place of business of the partnership, which is usually the general partner's ranch or business.

Always develop a statement of the purposes of the partnership, such as: "The partnership is engaged in the business of acquiring and standing at stud the Paint horse, Paint me Profits."

The division of profits and losses must be clearly stated. Each partner's profits or losses will be based on his percentage share of the total partnership. If the partner owns 10 per cent of the total partnership, then his division of profits should be 10 per cent, or his losses would be 10 per cent. A limited partner, however, cannot lose more than he has invested.

The compensation to the general partner for the work performed for the partnership should be clearly indicated. This is another way horses can make you money, so be sure you pay yourself adequately.

Also, be sure to include a statement that the general partner is NOT required to devote full-time effort and attention to the partnership.

The following is a bare bones sample of what a limited partnership agreement might include. You are welcome to use the information provided, but again, I warn you that making a public offering has many legal implications. You should have an attorney represent you.

The first step is to say who is taking part in the agreement (the general partner and the limited partners), and the date the agreement is being drafted.

The **first article** will define the partnership.

Include a statement of formation which will tell where the partnership is being established, the name of the partnership, the purpose of the partnership, the principle place of business and the term of the partnership. The partnership usually ends when the main asset of the partnership--the stallion--is sold or otherwise disposed.

Establish a list of definitions. Things to be included are the terms "agreement, adjusted invested capital account, assignee, cash available for distribution, general partner, limited partner, net income and loss, a substituted limited partner" and the term "vote."

The **second article** of the partnership names the general partner and outlines the obligations of the general partner, how the general partner might be replaced, how additional limited partners may be admitted, and what will be given each limited partner as evidence of his interest in the partnership. (Perhaps a certificate.)

The **third article** will explain the means of capitalization--total amount to be sought--the contributions by the general partner and the limited partners, and the method by which calls for additional capital may be made. This section should clearly state any interest which would be paid on contributions and whether or not there can be withdrawals or return of capital. Be sure to limit the distribution of any partnership property to "cash only" so the stallion cannot be taken out of your control. You will also want to make it understood the general partner can award a distribution of cash to partners whenever deemed reasonable, if cash available for distribution has been sufficiently generated through profits, sales, etc.

This is also the place to award the general partner immediate reimbursement for any and all expenses advanced for the partnership.

The **fourth article** can cover the allocation and distribution of profits and losses.

Here you must establish exactly what you will pay the general partner. If, for example, you want to get 30 per cent of the profits, take the 30 per cent off the top, then split the remaining money according to the percentage owned by each of the limited partners.

Remember, you are entitled, as the general partner, to be paid and paid handsomely for your ideas and efforts.

Don't limit the general partner. Make it possible for the general partner to be able to refinance or sell partnership assets to provide cash for distribution. Always keep the doors open for the general partner to be able to sell the stallion if a profit opportunity arises.

Article five can determine the latitude allowed the general partner in management.

The idea is to acquire a stallion and operate a financially successful breeding program, as well as other activities which the general partner feels would be advantageous to the partnership as a whole. Give the general partner plenty of room in which to operate, such as acquiring other property--horses, corrals, barns, land, etc.--selling of assets, or borrowing from third parties so additional money is available for allied investments.

Place restrictions on limited partners so it is difficult for them to take part directly or indirectly in the day-to-day business operations. You want the limited partners to promote the stallion with others and help make the operation profitable, but you don't want them in your way. Give the limited partners the right to act, is so desired, as a contractor, agent or employee of the partnership, to consult with the general partner, to act as surety for the partnership or guarantee one or more specific debts.

Be sure to include a statement that the limited partners authorize the general partner to act alone in acquiring property, entering contracts, arranging financing or completing other arrangements needed to reach the goals of the partnership.

You must make a generic statement regarding the standard by which the general partner conducts business. Say something like "unless fraud, deceit, or wrongful taking is involved," the general partner is not liable or obligated for mistakes resulting in any loss to the partnership or partners.

Make it difficult for the limited partners to remove the general partner.

Make removal based on cause, defined as dereliction of duty directly related to dishonesty, fraud, improper use of partnership assets, or self dealing to the detriment of the partnership. Require at least 75 per cent of the partnership to vote for removal at a general membership meeting which represents 100 per cent of the partnership shares.

The **sixth article** can deal with records and accounts.

Keep the partnership on a cash basis and close the accounts annually, making the fiscal year the same as the calendar year.

The required records, which should be kept at the general partner's office, will include a current list of all limited partners, a copy of the Certificate of Limited Partnership, if such exists, copies of the limited partnership's federal, state and local income tax information, copies of the agreement and amendments and financial statements.

It should be noted that upon request, any limited partner can get a copy of the records and he can inspect the records during normal business hours. The general partner should furnish financial statements on an annual basis, plus a report of progress when deemed necessary.

Of course the general partner must open a bank account in the name of the partnership. All partnership funds and no other funds shall be deposited into the account.

Article seven can define the rights, powers, duties and restrictions of the partners. It is important that the first section give the general partner the full and exclusive control over the management, conduct and operation of the partnership in all matters.

Again, the general partner should not be required to devote full time to the business, and again, a salary or form of compensation should be stated.

The limited partners should have voting rights on the following matters: a change in the nature of the partnership business, a transaction in which the general partner has a conflict of interest, the removal of the general partner, loans to the partnership, transacting business with the partnership and partners engaging in other business.

In **article eight** list all the requirements for meetings, such as notification, how a meeting can be called and where it can be held, what constitutes a quorum, requirements for limited partners to act and proxies.

You will need an explanation of how the general partner and the limited partners can assign or transfer their interests in the partnership. This can be tricky and legally sticky.

Normally, the general partner is not allowed to transfer or assign any interest in the partnership to anyone.

However, the best thing to do, in my opinion, is to keep it simple and say interests can only be transferred to family members.

A limited partner can, of course, sell his interest at any time, upon the approval of the general partner and the other limited partners. Requiring approval of the sale of an interest protects the other partners from being burdened with a partner they do not want for various reasons.

The death, bankruptcy or incompetence of a limited partner should not keep that partner or his heirs from all rights under the partnership.

Article nine might cover the liability of the partners. The liability of the general partner is usually unrestricted. The liability of the limited partners is restricted and limited to the amount of actual capital contribution each partner has made.

Partners should not be allowed to use the partnership name except in the ordinary course of the partnership business.

No partner should be allowed to disclose to any non-partner any of the partnership business practices, trade secrets or other information not publicly known. No partner should act contrary to the agreement or detrimentally to the success of the business or make it impossible for the partnership to carry on the business.

The general partner should not use any of the assets of the partnership, directly or indirectly, for any purpose other than the conduct of the partnership business.

There should be a section of indemnification in which the partnership agrees to act to protect the general partner if he were threatened, or named in a proceeding, and the partnership agrees to pay legal costs to protect the general partner.

The next article could cover the dissolution of the partnership which should take place when the purposes of the agreement have been met, or when the assets of the partnership have been sold.

The partnership could also be ended with the loss of the general partner, or by judicial decree.

You may wish to add a section in which it specifies the general partner is not obligated to tell the partnership about any other investment opportunities which might be available, and that the general partner has the right to take advantage of such opportunities. Frequently, during the normal course of doing partnership business, the general partner will be afforded the chance to participate in other profit centers. The right to do so should not be compromised.

End your agreement by stating that amendments may be made by a vote of the general partner and a majority interest of the limited partners entitled to vote. Any amendment shall be in writing, dated and executed by consenting partners.

Finally, state that the agreement contains the entire understanding of the partners and supersedes any prior written or oral agreements.

"There are no representations, agreements, arrangements or understandings, oral or written, between and among the partners relating to the subject matter of this agreement that are not fully expressed herein."

Once a limited partner signs the agreement and gives you his investment money, there can be little argument as to who is in charge, and that you have the right to conduct the business affairs as you see fit.

Using this guide you can, with some effort, write an agreement to serve your purposes.

Syndications are a good way to raise capital, a good way to be compensated for your efforts and an excellent way to make money with stallions.

Attachment to your expectations only brings grief. Let go of your attachments, and every effort is a success in itself.

Chapter eight
Look good, feel good makes money

I've saved this make-money chapter for last, since it details the one sure method of making money with horses. There are no "ifs", no "ands", no "buts", just income.

Train horses owned by someone else.

Win, lose, or draw, the trainer almost always gets paid. (There will be some hard-to-collect accounts, but not many if you are alert and maintain good business practices.) If the horse turns out to be a champion, the trainer gets paid, usually with a bonus. If the horse sells, or doesn't sell, if the horse lives, or dies, the trainer gets paid.

You may not get rich as a trainer, but you'll get paid.

If you have your own ideas, and you work hard, and you are dedicated to your craft, you'll make money. You might even become very wealthy. It's up to you.

Now if you do want to make a lot of money as a trainer, then all you have to do is play the game.

You don't have to be the greatest trainer in the world to make money. You don't even have to be good.

But you do have to know how the game is played, and the very best ways to accumulate the big bucks.

I wouldn't presume to tell you how to train a horse.

There are as many ways to train a horse as there are trainers. Every horse is an individual, needing special care and attention in the development of his or her special skills.

You may wish to train trotting horses, or jumpers, or race horses, or western pleasure horses. You decide what you want to train and how you want to train. It really doesn't matter, just as long as you know and follow the rule by which horses can make a trainer a lot of money.

The one and only absolute rule: always make your customers "look good" and "feel good".

Trainers who make money know they really only have two major functions. Neither involves training a horse. Trainers who make money dedicate the vast majority of their time working on these two most important jobs.

1. A trainer must attract more customers, increasing total income.

2. A trainer must find new and better ways to increase the margin between effort and profits.

Attracting customers--the ones who pay the bills and provide the profits--is priority one.

A key element of good marketing is distribution. You must get the goods or services to the customer. Or, you must get the customer to the goods or services.

If you aren't already in the middle of the market which wants a trainer for the kind of horse you want to train, then you must find that market, and go to it. If you want to train race horses, go to the race track. If you want to train jumpers, locate in an area where jumpers are the number one topic of conversation. Sure, you might have to pick up and move lock, stock and barrel. But you'll do it because it's part of the make-money game.

Don't attempt to train dressage horses in the heart of cutting horse country, or run Quarter Horses in a state where there is no Quarter Horse racing. Look for an abundance of the kind of horses you want to train. And don't worry about there being too many trainers in the area already; few of them will know or follow the "look good, feel good" rule to becoming a wealthy trainer.

The customers of other trainers will soon be your customers because you will attract customers, and you will make them "look good" and "feel good".

Nothing breeds success like success.

And one of the best ways to "show off" your success and ability is to get an education. You don't have to do a thing to impress potential customers if you have the "credentials to show you have the knowledge." There are so few horse trainers with formal education within their field that you will stand head and shoulders above most of your competition.

There are more than 200 colleges in the U.S. today which have two or four-year Equine Science programs. If there is no college near you, there are colleges with online courses. Success Is Easy presents an online course, Training Performance Horses, which is open entry and work at your own pace. The nine-lesson course is offered by four different colleges, each of which presents the student with a certificate of recognition when the course is completed. That's a great way to start.

Survey after survey has concluded that **incomes increase substantially** for those with some sort of formal education.

It's easy to let prospective customers know about your educational background, and when they do, they expect to pay.

Being successful in school is one of the best ways a trainer can attract new customers.

Your education accomplishments is an image of success that carries over into all facets of your business.

To attack new customers you don't have to be the world's greatest trainer. You don't even have to have a winning record in competitions.

But you must always be sure your customer "looks good and feel good" when they are with you. They must "look good and feel good" about the things they are doing, or learning or simply enjoying. You must be sure your customers want to be involved in the activities you create at your training facility. One happy customer attracts others.

Look good and feel good means never having a customer look bad or feel bad.

Never, never tell a customer his pride and joy or her precious baby can't win, can't run or can't jump. You never, never tell a customer a thing like that unless you've suddenly developed a phobia about making money. If you want to make money, you must have horses--so no matter how bad the horse is, you still have to make the customer "look good" and "feel good." Remember, no matter how bad a horse is, he's always better than an empty stall.

Never, never fail to tell an owner the truth about his or her horse. A customer who has been lied to never looks good or feels good. Every horse has plenty of positive aspects to talk about. Talk about how full the glass, not how empty.

You know that only a small percentage of horses are winners at anything, yet their owners love them dearly. So making an owner look good and feel good about the horse he or she loves isn't that big a problem. It just takes some positive thought.

A trainer who is making money is thinking his or her way to increased profit margins and increased income. A trainer who is making money finds a way to make an owner look good and feel good. And there are lots of ways to do that without seeking head to head combat in the show ring or other venues.

Study each of your new customers or your potential customers. What makes each of them look good and feel good? It will probably be a different thing for each, but for all, there are some basic steps to follow.

First, be a good horseman and dedicate yourself to improving every day. Give horse training your very best efforts. Your attitude and efforts will be noticed and appreciated by your customers, and they will feel good being associated with you.

Now add some creative profit thinking.

Matching stall signs, matching halters, matching blankets, matching name plates, matching tack trunks give a "team" appearance to a shed row. It makes customers' horses look good, and customers feel good. And there is always a little profit for the trainer when such items are purchased through regular sources.

Being a part of a team is very important to most of us. It is that feeling of "acceptance" which all humans crave. So when your barn makes everyone feel part of something important, they want to stay and they are willing to pay. Don't be afraid to charge well for your services. It's part of the game.

Some creative trainers are very well paid because they are very good baby-sitters.

Their entire training service is really just baby-sitting the horseowner's children.

If you keep the little darlings happy, impressively attired and on a flashy horse, the mom, pop and the kid will look good and feel good, no matter the results of the competition.

Now if you really want to make a lot of money, and you are really thinking of ways to increase profit margins and total income, you'll find a way to take the child to a level of competition at which he or she can win. Maybe on a horse you just sold to them....one with potential. You know how to find and sell a horse with potential, don't you?

Winning at the smallest backyard show makes mom and pop look and feel great. The kid's a star, and you're on your way to the bank with a bigger roll.

Don't knock it. Baby-sitting trainers--and that's the majority--do extremely well with poor stock and no training talent. They attract customers and they increase income and profit by making everyone look good and feel good.

If you are a decorating genius, you can get rich just by applying your non-training ideas. The "status-ego" of some horseowners can keep you in the chips if you dress the part and see to it the horses look the part.

A friend once told me, "Customers can see the shine on a horse, but they can't see the time and training in one." He was correct. He was also wealthy.

Glossy horses, standing in clean stalls, with personal rub rags and brushes in the tack trunks with embossed name plates, impress the current owners and attract new customers.

Many people will pay anything to be part of an exclusive club. Without doubt, they believe they look good, and they know they feel good when they tell their friends how much extra they have to pay just to be in your stable. Some very profit-oriented trainers insist their clients buy special saddles and equipment, for which they get handsome kickbacks.

It costs plenty to join some private clubs, and there is almost always a waiting list. (Waiting lists are another good way to attract customers. I know one fellow who makes everyone wait at least 30 days before they can get into his stable. He claims it gives him time to learn just how much a prospective customer is willing to spend on horses and equipment.)

In those kinds of barns, who cares about winning? Those owners have the very best for their horse. And the trainer has the profits.

If you are training competitive horses, but not winning regularly, you really never have to make excuses for poor performances by any horse. If you think about it, whether it's a race horse, show horse, or pleasure riding horse, the owner will give you all the excuses ever needed if you just keep quiet. The owner will think of a hundred reasons to continue to pay you to train that special horse.

Shuffle your feet and kick the dirt, or continue grooming the horse, but don't speak. The owner will provide an explanation soon enough for why the horse misbehaved, or didn't win. Then all you have to do is agree with the owner, and the owner looks good and feels good.

If I've seen it once, I've seen it hundreds of times. A dirty, rotten, no-good spoiled horse will dump, kick, or somehow hurt an owner, and the owner will immediately explain why it wasn't the horse's fault.

Want to make money? Just listen, don't argue and don't criticize. If you let the owner look good and feel good, he'll be happy as a clam, continue to pay, and probably buy another dink for five times what he's worth. And if the trainer sells that new dink, it's even more money for the trainer.

Be cool. Let the owner enjoy his or her horse, and the money will come rolling in.

It takes no horsemanship ability at all to be a wealthy trainer. Anyone who follows the rule can be a very wealthy trainer. Horses can make you rich.

Now don't misunderstand. There are a lot of wealthy trainers who have loads of ability and horsemanship talent. It's just that they didn't become rich on training skills alone. In addition to being gifted, they know and follow the plan. They attract customers--on skills and winning records, too--and they find ways to increase profit margins and boost income.

For trainers, there are many avenues to a pot of gold.

Trainers have more opportunities than anyone else to take advantage of the other methods you've already learned. It's simply because trainers are more often in the right place at the right time.

For example, training facilities are an excellent way to "land bank", and make money.

Horse facilities are usually located in an area not really suited to other commercial ventures. The land is normally less expensive. So while you are making money practicing your trade as a trainer, the land you are utilizing is appreciating in value. Just as every horse you have is for sale, so is the land.

You would be surprised how may horse-owning customers will be interested in purchasing your gold mine if you just suggest to them that it is for sale.

Just as there is always another horse, there is always another place--especially if the profit margin will help make you rich.

If you don't wish to, or can't afford to start a land bank, then lease the facilities needed for your business, or go to a public stable. The advantages of doing this are many.

First, most of your new customers are already there. Horseowners love to switch from a trainer who doesn't make them look good or feel good to a trainer who does. It's a fact that you'll take your good customers with you and pick up new ones every time you change locations. (Some trainers do change locations every time they want to add new customers.) Make your section of the public facility the fanciest. You'll have people stopping by just to smell the roses. And it shouldn't surprise you when they decide to join you.

Second, your income generally remains constant with your costs. If you need 20 stalls for paying customers, your costs are proportionate. If the number of stalls needed goes down, so do your costs.

Third, you'll have more time to practice your craft, which is attracting customers, making customers look good and feel good, and thinking of new and better ways to make more money. After all, at a leased facility, you don't have to spend your valuable time fixing and repairing all the little problems so common to a training stable.

Remember, the only three ways of making money with horses is to "win purses", "sell horses" and sell your potential to make the owners look good and feel good.

Don't be afraid to call on every horse owner that is the kind of person you want in your barn. Yes, you will step on some toes taking customers from others. But believe me, the guy who protests the most about you won't hesitate to accept one of your clients. And no matter how hard you try, you will lose some customers. Smile as you wave good-by, the potential for your success is unlimited.

Horses--what a great way to get wealthy!

You can start with very little money, and get sizable returns on your investment. You can start with a lot of money and still get impressive returns on your investment.

You can participate in one, or any number of facets of the horse industry, and get wealthy.

You can do the thing you love best, and make money doing it.

But everything isn't always roses. Life doesn't work that way, and neither does the horse industry.

I've told you how to make money with horses. The surest way to lose money with horses is to own more than you should. If horses are your business, then make something else your hobby.

Winning and selling make money.

Owning a horse for the pure pleasure is an expense.

Own one, maybe two. But own many and you will be "horse poor". I guarantee it.

Those are the rules. Following them is certainly the toughest part of being successful.

Following the rules means lots and lots of study, effort and dedication.

But you can do it.

And you can make money with horses.

Concentration is the key to your economic results.

Chapter nine
Horsemen get tax benefits

Once you make a lot of money with horses, you'll have to look for ways to shelter and invest your money. You don't want to be in a higher tax bracket without having a way to protect your new wealth.

With half of all income over $50,000 per year going for federal income tax, the average person must take advantage of the methods by which the Internal Revenue Service (IRS) has made it possible to ease the tax burden.

Horsemen are especially lucky, and should investigate the tax benefits available. Instead of considering horse ownership as a pleasurable past time, look upon it as a business pursuit. While the pleasure is always there, all that is necessary to have your cake and eat it too is the intent or expectation of making a profit.

Some of the prerequisites, of course, are that the horse operation be treated as a legitimate business. Enlisting professional help, keeping proper records and handling the books as in any other business are basic. Establishing plans, goals, and budgets will help prove the business intent and profit motive.

The IRS has made it easy to meet the first requirement. You only have to show a profit in any two of seven consecutive years to establish a profit motive. In some cases, even this requirement can be waived, provided you do have a legitimate business, profit intentions, and the reasonable possibility of attaining your goals. The profit-making plans in this book, if you have records to show you followed them, prove your intentions. But if you don't make a profit in seven years, you must have adequate records, evidence and the willingness to face legal action to protect your tax deductions.

Another important assistance offered to horsemen by the IRS is the useful life expectancy table for race horses, broodmares, and stallions at stud. These guidelines are quite liberal, and with any luck at all, the odds are definitely in favor of the horseman. These guides were established after intensive study by industry experts and are accepted without question by the IRS.

For instance, the useful life of breeding stock is considered to be 16 years. However, you know of many mares and stallions which go on much longer. Something Royal, dam of Secretariat, was 18 years old when she foaled him. She had her final foal at age 25. Count Fleet was 20 when he sired his last foals.

Because of these guidelines, a person in the horse business can often recover the full cost of horses through depreciation, and still have the profit-producing horse for many years.

An example: instead of buying young mares with potential to resell, invest in older proven mares for tax advantages.

By taking advantage of the tax laws, you can depreciate the full purchase price of the mare over the minimum holding period of 24 months. Therefore, a 14-year-old mare in foal will have her cost recovered in tax deductions in two years, and the owner will still have the foal (maybe two) and the mare.

CHART A

Age Acquired	------------Useful Life------------------		
	Colts & Fillies	Geldings	Stallions & Broodmares
1 year	5 years	6 years	------------
2 years	4 years	5 years	------------
3 years	3 years	4 years	10 years
4 years	2 years	3 years	10 years
5 years	24 months	24 months	10 years
6 years	24 months	24 months	10 years
7 years	-------	---------	9 years
8 years	-------	---------	8 years
9 years	-------	---------	7 years
10 years	-------	---------	6 years
11 years	-------	---------	5 years
12 years	-------	---------	4 years
13 years	-------	---------	3 years
14 years	-------	---------	24 months
Older	-------	---------	24 months

Chart A--depreciation for horses--shows the total investment in your horse can be fully recovered through depreciation. The method to use must be determined by individual circumstances. As some methods can be very complicated, a tax accountant familiar with the horse business should be consulted. The methods to ask about include straight line, declining balance, and sum of the years digits.

Careful consideration of your particular position should be made before choosing any method other than straight line. Once the selection of a method is made, it becomes very difficult to change. Permission must be obtained from the IRS, and in some cases, a change could be prohibited for up to 10 years.

The following charts outline some examples of depreciation on weanlings, unbroken yearlings, and mares. (Note: the yearlings, except geldings, do not qualify for additional first year depreciation, and the mares do not qualify for sum of the years digits, declining balance or additional first year if 11-years-old, or older. Check each year to make sure there are no changes in these rules.)

CHART B

14-YEAR-OLD BROODMARE OR STALLION
COST $20,000
2-YEAR USEFUL LIFE

	Straight line
First year	$10,000
Second year	$10,000
Total cost fully recovered	$20,000

In the case of a yearling or a race horse taken out of training before he or she is fully depreciated, then converted to breeding purposes, the remaining undepreciated value would be depreciated over the useful "breeding" life.

CHART   C

SIX-YEAR-OLD BROODMARE OR STALLION
COST $20,000
10 YEAR USEFUL LIFE

Straight line with additional first year depreciation.

	Depreciation	Single, corp., partner return	Joint Return
First year	$2,000	$3,800*	$5,600**
Second	2,000	1,800	1,600
Years three through 10	$2,000	$1,800	$1,600
	$20,000	$20,000	$20,000

*First year additional depreciation computation limited to $10,000 of investment.

**First year additional depreciation limited to $20,000 of investment.

Tax laws are constantly changing, so keep in mind it is important to be aware of updates. The American Horse Council, in Washington D. C., has conducted tax workshops, and in the past, has published valuable reference material on taxes and the horseman.

CHART D

YEARLING DEPRECIATION
COST $20,000
5 YEAR USEFUL LIFE

	Straight Line	Sum of Years Digits	Double Declining Balance
First year	$4,000	$6,667	$8,000
Second year	4,000	5,333	4,800
Third year	4,000	4,000	2,880
Fourth year	4,000	2,667	1,728
Fifth year	4,000	1,333	2,592
	$20,000	$20,000	$20,000

If you conduct your horse business as a business, you'll gain many tax advantages simply from legitimate business expenses.

Business motor vehicles are a good example. If you have a car which you use for both business and pleasure, the business cost of operations and repairs is deductible. But if you have two cars, make one of them a business truck, then all the operational costs are a legitimate expense, and you have no problem with the division of expenses. The cost of a motor vehicle bought for use in your business must actually be capitalized, but if you lease a truck, all the cost is deductible. The same applies to a horse trailer.

Tools, machinery and equipment are deductible business expenses provide they are short-lived, wear out, or are thrown away within one year.

Memberships, dues to horse organizations, subscriptions to horse magazines and technical books on horses (such as this one, and our monthly Make Money Newsletter) are deductible expenses.

You may also deduct amounts spent for your own education in your trade, business or profession, along with certain related travel, including meals and lodging. To qualify, you must show the education maintains or improves the skills required in your business. But then we all know no one ever stops learning about horses.

Some personal expenses become deductible once you establish that horses are your business.

If you rent a large home and property and have a gardener to mow the lawn, you have no deductions. But if you have horses on the property, a portion of the rent is now deductible. If the gardener is contracted instead as a groom, you have another deductible expense.

If you set aside a room in the house for an office, you can take another portion of the rent as a deduction, along with a portion of the light bill, heat and telephone bills, and the cost of desks, tables, chairs, paper, ink, adding machines, etc.

The catch, however, is that you must be able to show all business expenses were **ordinary** and **necessary** and directly connected with the operation of your business.

Depreciation and the reduction of taxable income by the simple addition of legitimate business expenses are two of the main ways a horseman can benefit from tax laws.

A horseman can also "shelter" income by investing in horses, especially race horses.

But you must be careful.

Most so-called tax shelters are sold on the basis of deliberately having a loss in one operation to offset income from another. That's dishonest and not legal.

Uncle Sam is a nice guy, and he says if you want to be partners with him in a business, that's okay with him. He says if you make money, then you share fifty-fifty. (Tax shelters are really only good for high tax bracket people--50 per cent rate.) But if you lose money, then Uncle Sam will pay for half the loss, provided you have other income from which to deduct the loss.

Now that's very fair of Uncle Sam. Tax shelters should be just as fair.

But most tax shelters are designed to keep from paying Uncle Sam his share when winning, and making him pay for losses, even when you actually benefit in some way. And that's not right.

Usually the shelter is set up to load a lot of expense with little or no income into the first two or three years of operation. Then as the startup costs are gradually absorbed, and the operation becomes profitable, the shelter promoter sells the investor out, paying taxes at a long term capital gain rate instead of at ordinary income rates. The investor then puts the proceeds of the sellout into a new shelter and the pyramid goes on.

In any case, unless there is downright fraud, Uncle Sam is supposed to get paid sometime. He doesn't mind tax minimizing, in fact, it's encouraged. But tax evasion is illegal. You cannot make money legitimately by losing money. If you attempt to do so, you violate the first rule of the IRS: there must be a profit motive. There are legitimate ways to avoid tax consequences, defer, and/or minimize taxes. But they all involve eventual gain, not losses.

The Individual Retirement Accounts (IRAs) are a good example. With an investment in one you can avoid paying tax on current interest income, and on a limited amount of other income you invest. When you do withdraw the investment, it will then be income to you, and you will have to pay the taxes you deferred when you invested. However, the tax rate should then be considerable lower, due to your age and the probable absence of other income. Such accounts combine avoidance, deferment and minimizing--a good deal.

So look closely at any shelter offered you, even an investment in horses. There is bound to be a day of reckoning, one way or another. There is no free lunch!

The two mainstays of legitimate operations are depreciation and interest on borrowed money. Both are allowable deductions, and a major factor in cash flow. Depreciation gives you an expense item without using any cash, and borrowing for the operation gives you a larger capital base without the input of your own cash.

A good legal operation is investment in race horses.

The potential for profit--big, big, profit--is there. The intention to make money is there, and there is no question racing horses is a business.

Suppose you borrow $19,000 at 12 per cent simple interest, put up $1,000 of your own money, and buy a 2-year-old race horse, a filly. To qualify for recovery property with a present class life of three years, a race horse must be two years old, or older, when placed in service. It doesn't matter what the previous owner did tax wise; the filly is new to you, so you're entitled to recover the full cost.

Timing can be important, as the mere placing in service qualifies for a full year of depreciation, even if it should be on the last day of the year.

However, that's a judgment call you'll have to make depending on racing opportunities in your area.

For the purposes of the upcoming example, we'll just use the full years of her three, four and five-year-old years.

Earnings are also very important, but I'll not clutter up the example by speculating on them. The filly is bound to earn some money--you bought a race horse, not a slow horse, and you know how to read a catalog. Earnings can be eliminated without affecting the example.

A very simple basic three-year chart illustrates what can be achieved without resorting to anything illegal or questionable.

The chart assumes no change in her racing ability, broodmare potential, or any unforeseen accidents, circumstances, or tax law changes.

The figures, of course, are not actual. They could, and undoubtedly would, vary. The figures only demonstrate the possibilities of the leverage from depreciation and borrowing.

No earnings are assumed.

TAX SHELTERS
FIRST YEAR

Deductible Expenses	Cash Outlay
$5,000 Maintenance	$1,000 down payment
$5,000 Depreciation	$5,000 maintenance
$2,280 Interest on loan	$6,350 principal paid
	$2,280 loan interest
$12,280 total deductible	$14,630 cash out
resulting in .... $ 6,140 tax saving

$ 8,490 cash outlay

SECOND YEAR

$5,000 Maintenance	$5,000 maintenance
$7,600 Depreciation	$6,350 principal paid
$1,518 Interest on loan	$1,518 loan interest
$14,118 total deductible	$12,868 gross cash out
resulting in.............$7,059 cash tax saving

$5,809 net cash outlay

THIRD YEAR

Deductible Expense	Cash outlay
$5,000 maintenance	$5,000 maintenance
$7,400 Depreciation	$6,300 principal paid
$ 756 Interest	$ 756 loan interest
$13,156 total deductible	$12,056 cash expense

resulting in................ $6,578 cash tax saving
                                    $5,478 cash outlay

While no earnings have been assumed, the average earnings for a Quarter Horse of the caliber purchased at the example level are approximately $15,000 per year. Assuming earnings of that amount, you would still end up owning the horse without it costing you a cent for the investment. (Earnings of $45,000, less expenses of $39,554, equals a gain of $5,446, less tax liability of $2,723, equals a net gain of $2,723.)

Of course, the horse might turn out to be really great, earning hundreds of thousands, and then you'll have a new tax problem

The purpose of all this is to point out you don't need some questionable tax shelter when there are sound investment opportunities available.

Go for a profit, not a loss. And if you make it, be happy to see Uncle Sam gets his share.

Now go do it!

You can make a lot of money with your own horse business.

Afterword

We gain great knowledge by reading, but we learn best by doing. Once you have spent your money on a horse, you will learn quickly all the things you missed before purchasing. You may violate a rule you have read, but you will seldom violate the rule again if it is your money on the line.

Making mistakes is part of the process, and it is only by failure that you will eventually succeed. You never accomplish anything untried.

You have the ability within to achieve anything you can conceive. If you love horses and working with them, and you choose to make them your business, then dedicate yourself to the tasks and you will release your creative power and turn your dreams into reality.

You have special talents, and when you use those talents, you accomplish things easily. Apply your unique talents to making money with horses, and you will discover Success Is Easy.

Don Blazer

Whatever horsemen do with horses, Don has probably done. He isn't one to sit on fences just talking. He chooses to be a part of the action.

He's trained and ridden everything from top race horses to mustangs, and he's shown Western and English pleasure horses, reining horses, jumpers and dressage horses.

He's taught for seven colleges and universities and he's traveled from Australia to Alaska demonstrating training techniques. He instructs an online horse training course offered by four colleges.

Author of the internationally syndicated column, **A Horse, Of Course** and the monthly newsletter, **It's All About Money,** his advice and help are must reading for thousands of fans.

Of course he makes his money with horses four ways, as a trainer, author, trader and teacher. So the advice he offers here is more than just causal chatter; it is a report on the business of horses by a man who is in the business of horses.

When not at the typewriter, Don enjoys free time with his wife, Diane and their three horses, Walter, Katy and Dooley. The Blazers live in Scottsdale, AZ.

Making it and Saving it

IT'S ALL ABOUT MONEY

Published by Success Is Easy   Vol. 1   Issue No. 1   2002

Here it is at last, a monthly newsletter for all horsemen who want to own their own business, want to supplement their incomes, enjoy a better lifestyle, and have more money in their saddlebags.

It's All About Money is all about how horses can make your rich.   It's all about turning your love of horses into more dollars in your bank account. It's all about knowing how to save and where to save and when to save. (You'll love the section on upcoming product sales, special offers and freebies exclusively for subscribers.)

It's All About Money is all about knowing what you must know to increase profit margins, avoid down side risks and being on the inside when dollars count.

It's All About Money brings you the best in-depth interviews and profit-making advice from the experts.

It's All About Money brings you personality profiles of the people who lead the way and set the trends.

It's All About Money brings you insider tricks and tips for increasing profits, saving money, and investing in broodmares and stallions.

Subscribe Now!

You Can Make Money With Horses, But It Takes Action By You!

$24

Order online: **www.donblazer.com**

Annual subscription

Checks to: Success Is Easy, 7119 Shea , Scottsdale, AZ 85254 Designate Newsletter to be sent by e-mail or postal service. Be sure to provide e-mail and postal service addresses.

Natural Western Riding

THE ULTIMATE HORSE/RIDER PARTNERSHIP

Don Blazer gives you every rein position, every leg aid, every weight shift cue and every footfall sequence for every exercise. Endorsed by trainers. Bigger and better than ever, revised and updated, this is the book which set the standard for Western riding for more than 25 years. Now it leads the way into a new century; clear and comprehensive.

SPECIAL FEATURE

Cathy Hanson guides you step-by-step as you and your horse master trail courses.

$24.95   Order online: www.donblazer.com

Checks to: Success Is Easy, 7119 E. Shea Blvd. Ste. 109-271, Scottsdale, AZ 85254